THE JEWISH WIFE

Works of Bertolt Brecht
published by Grove Press

Baal, A Man's a Man, and *The Elephant Calf*
Edward II
Galileo
The Jewish Wife and Other Short Plays
Jungle of Cities and Other Plays
Manual of Piety
The Mother
Mother Courage and Her Children
The Threepenny Opera

BERTOLT BRECHT

THE JEWISH WIFE
And Other Short Plays

English versions by
ERIC BENTLEY

Grove Press
New York

Grove Press
841 Broadway
New York, NY 10003

CAUTION: These plays are fully protected, in whole, in part, or in
any form, under the copyright laws of the United States of America,
the British Empire, including Canada, and all other countries of the
Copyright Union, and are subject to royalty. Amateur and stock
rights on all these plays are held by Samuel French, Inc., 45 West
25th Street, New York, NY 10010. Questions about any musical
scores can also be addressed to Samuel French, Inc. Permission to
perform all or part of any of these scripts in any way, including
readings, must be obtained before rehearsals start or public an-
nouncements are made.

Salzburg Dance of Death and its Introduction first appeared in
Portfolio No. 8 and are reprinted by permission of *Art News*.

Library of Congress Cataloging-in-Publication Data

Brecht, Bertolt, 1898–1956.
    The Jewish wife and other short plays/Bertolt Brecht; English
versions by Eric Bentley.—1st Evergreen ed.
      p.   cm.
    Includes bibliographical references (p.   ).
    Contents: The Jewish wife—In search of justice—The
informer—The elephant calf—The measures taken—The exception and the rule—Appendix: Salzburg dance of death—
Appendix: What was he killed for?
    ISBN 0-8021-5098-5
    1. Brecht, Bertolt, 1898–1956—Translations, English. I. Title.
PT2603.R397A22   1992   91-34823
832′.912—dc20

Manufactured in the United States of America

First Edition 1965
First Evergreen Edition 1992

10 9 8 7 6 5 4 3 2

CONTENTS

Foreword   7

The Jewish Wife   9

In Search of Justice   19

The Informer   41

The Elephant Calf
  or, The provability of any and every
  contention   57

The Measures Taken   75

The Exception and the Rule   109

Appendix: Salzburg Dance of Death   145

Appendix: What Was He Killed For?   159

Bibliographical Notes   173

FOREWORD

THE SHORT PLAYS in this book have been chosen, not as treatments of a common theme or examples of a common method — they exhibit neither — , but for convenience in reading and in producing. Here is Brecht for the bedside table and the community theatre. Suffice it, then, merely to identify each play.

The Jewish Wife, In Search of Justice, and *The Informer* are all scenes from that chronicle of life under the Nazis on which Brecht worked during the middle thirties. As tales of horror, they seem mild after the news of later years. Yet the virus is there, and the diagnosis is correct, even if the disease is not depicted at its height.

Brecht's miniatures of monstrosity have their special value and his peculiar signature. Just as the "optimistic" *Lehrstuecke* have tragic undertones, so the "tragic" chronicle of the Third Reich is at the same time a comedy. We can hardly feel sorry for Judge A: we must find him grotesque, comic. The same with the schoolmaster in *The Informer*. And actresses who play the Jewish wife exclusively for pathos have failed to notice that, like Judge A and the schoolmaster, this woman is asking: "Why is this happening to *me* — I always went along?" Her fate is neither tragic nor purely pathetic: it is ironic, grotesque, almost ridiculous, and therefore only one step from the funny. . . . It is for such reasons that these Brechtian scenes still live on the stage while the rest of the "progressive" drama of the thirties, including some scenes from this very chronicle of Brecht's, now seems antediluvian.

The Elephant Calf was written as a kind of appendix to Brecht's comedy *A Man's A Man.* Such mystery as it may contain will be dispelled, I believe, by a reading

7

of the longer play. Others believe it is intended to remain mysterious. (Martin Esslin has taken this position in his book on Brecht; I have ventured to dissent in the Grove Press edition of *Baal, A Man's A Man and The Elephant Calf.*)

The Measures Taken, in its full panoply of a Hanns Eisler score, is a kind of secular, or counter-religious, oratorio. Without the music it is a one act play — some would say a one act tragedy. (Some of Brecht's comments on the play are cited in my *The Modern Theatre,* Volume Six. And again Martin Esslin has pertinent comments in his book.)

The Exception and the Rule, like *The Measures Taken,* is what Brecht called a *Lehrstueck* — a didactic piece. Both Paul Dessau and Stefan Wolpe have composed scores for it. Also like *The Measures Taken,* it could at first be taken as a product of Marxian optimism. But, once again like *The Measures Taken,* there is a countervailing tragic element. (Perhaps one does not bear in mind, at a first reading of the trial scene, that the Coolie had not offered water to the Merchant from humane motives.)

— ERIC BENTLEY, NEW YORK, 1964

THE JEWISH WIFE

CHARACTERS

The Wife

The Husband

It is evening. A woman is packing. She is picking out the things she wants to take with her. Sometimes she takes an article out of the bag again and puts it back in its place so that she can pack something else. She hesitates a long time over a large picture of her husband which is on the dressing table. In the end she leaves it where it is. Getting tired of packing, she sits for a few moments on a suitcase, her head propped on her hand. Then she goes to the telephone.

WIFE: Judith Keith speaking. Is that you, doctor? Good evening. — I just wanted to call and say you'll have to be looking for a new bridge partner. Yes, I'm going away. — No, not for very long, but not less than a couple of weeks. I'm going to Amsterdam. — Yes, they say the spring is lovely there. — I have friends there. — No, friends, in the plural, unbelievable as it sounds. — How can you play bridge now? But we haven't played for two weeks. — Certainly, Fritz had a cold too. When it gets so cold, bridge is impossible, I said so too. — Oh no, doctor, how could I? — Thekla had to accommodate her mother. — I know. — How should I suppose *that?* — No, it really didn't come suddenly at all, it's just that I kept putting it off, but now I must . . . Yes, we'll have to call off our movie date. Say hello to Thekla for me. — Perhaps you'll call him sometimes on Sundays? So long then. — Well, gladly, of course. — Good-bye.

She hangs up and calls another number.

Judith Keith speaking. I'd like to speak to Frau Shoeck. — Lotte? — I wanted to say a quick goodbye, I'm going away for a time. — No, I'm quite well, I just want to see a couple of new faces. —

11

Yes, what I wanted to say was that Fritz is bringing the professor here for the evening next Tuesday, and perhaps you could come too. As I said, I'm leaving tonight. — Yes, Tuesday. — No, I only wanted to say I'm leaving tonight, that has nothing to do with it, I thought you could come then too. — All right, let's say: *although* I'm not there, shall we? — Of course I know you're not like that and, even if you were, these are troubled times, and everybody's careful. You'll come then? — If Max can? Oh, he will be able to, the professor'll be here, tell him. — I must hang up now. Fine. Good-bye.

She hangs up and calls another number.

Is that you, Gertrude? This is Judith. Sorry to disturb you. — Thanks. I wanted to ask you if you can look after Fritz, I'm going away for a couple of months. — I think that you as his sister . . . Why wouldn't you like to? — But there's no likelihood of that, not in Fritz's case. Naturally he knows that — or — you and I didn't get on too well together, but . . . Then *he'll* call *you* if you wish it. — Yes, I'll tell him. — It's all pretty much in order, though the apartment's a bit too big. — His study? Oh, Ida knows how to look after it, just leave 'that to her. — I find her quite intelligent, and he's used to her. — And another thing, please don't misunderstand me, he doesn't like to talk before dinner, would you remember that? I've always avoided it. — I don't want to discuss it now, my train leaves soon and I've not finished packing, you see. — Look after his suits and remind him he has to go to the tailor — he's ordered a coat — and take care that his bedroom's well heated, he always sleeps with an open window and it's too cold. — I don't believe he should "become inured" to it, but now I must stop. — Thank you so much, Gertrude, and we'll write each other. — Good-bye.

She hangs up and calls another number.

Anna? This is Judith. Look, I'm leaving right away.
— No, it has to be, it's getting too difficult — too
difficult! Yes, no, Fritz. *doesn't* want it, he knows
nothing. I simply packed. — I don't think so. — I
don't think he'll say much. — It's simply too hard
for him, I mean, too many technicalities. — We
never discussed it. — We never even spoke about
it, never. — No, he was *not* different, on the contrary — I want you to be good to him a little at
first. — Yes, especially Sundays, and advise him to
move. — The apartment is too big for him. — I'd
like to say good-bye to you, but you know — the
superintendent?* — Good-bye then. No, don't come
to the station, by no means. Good-bye, I'll write. —
Surely.

*She hangs up and calls no more numbers. She has
been smoking. She now burns the little book in which
she looked up the telephone numbers. She walks
up and down a couple of times. Then she begins
to speak. She is trying out the little speech she
wishes to make to her husband. One sees that he
is supposed to be in a certain chair.*

Yes, I'm going now, Fritz. Perhaps I've stayed too
long already; you must forgive me, but . . .

She stands thinking and then tries again.

Fritz, you shouldn't keep me any longer, you
can't. . . . It's clear I'll be your undoing. I know
you're not cowardly, you're not afraid of the police
—but there are worse things than the police. They
won't take you to a concentration camp but —
tomorrow or the next day — they'll exclude you from
the clinic. You won't say anything then, but you'll be
sick. I refuse to see you sitting around here turning

---

* She means he is a Nazi.

the pages of magazines. I'm going out of pure selfishness and nothing else. Don't say anything.

She stops again. And tries again.

Don't say you're not changed. You are! Last week you found — "quite objectively" — that the percentage of Jewish scientists is after all not so great. It always begins with objectivity. And why are you always telling me I was "never such a nationalist as today." Naturally! It's so catching! Oh Fritz, what has happened to us?

She pauses.

I didn't tell you I wanted to go, and *have* wanted to go a long time, because I can't talk when I look at you, Fritz. Talking seems so futile. They've fixed everything. What's wrong with them? What do they want actually? What do I do to them? I've never meddled in politics. Was I for Thaelmann? * No, I'm thoroughly bourgeois, a housewife with servants and so forth, and now suddenly only blondes can do this sort of thing. I've often thought lately how you said years ago: "There are valuable people and less valuable people. The valuable people get insulin when they have sugar in the blood, the less valuable don't." I agreed with you. Well, now they've made new categories of this sort, and I belong to the less valuable. It serves me right.

Another pause.

Yes, I'm packing. You mustn't act as if you hadn't noticed in the last few days . . . Fritz, everything is tolerable except one thing: that we're not looking each other in the eyes during the last hour that remains to us. That they shall not achieve — the liars who set everyone lying. Ten years ago when

* Communist leader.

somebody thought no one could tell I was Jewish you quickly said: "Oh, yes, they can tell." And I liked that. It was clearheaded. Why evade the issue now? I'm packing because otherwise they'll take away your position as chief surgeon at the clinic. And because they already cut you there to your face and because already you can't sleep at night. I don't want you to tell me not to go. I'm going in a hurry because I don't want to have you tell me I *should* go. It's a question of time. Character is a question of time. It lasts for a certain length of time, just like a glove. There are good ones that last a long time. But they don't last forever. Incidentally, I'm *not* angry. And yet: I am. Why should I always be so understanding? What's wrong with the shape of my nose and the color of my hair? They want me to leave the town where I was born so they won't have to provide for me. What kind of men are you all? What kind of a man are you? You people discover the quantum theory and let yourselves be bossed by half-savages; you have to conquer the world for them, but you're not allowed to have the wife you want. Artificial respiration and every shot a hit! You're monsters or the bootlickers of monsters. Yes, this is unreasonable of me, but what use is reason in such a world? There you sit, watching your wife pack and you say nothing. The walls have ears, don't they? And you all say nothing? One lot listen and the other lot hold their tongues. God! I should hold my tongue too. If I loved you, I'd hold my tongue. I love you, really. Give me that underwear. Those have sex appeal, I'll need them. I'm thirty-six, that's not too old, but I can't do much more experimenting. It mustn't be this way in the next country I come to. The next man I get must be allowed to keep me. And don't say you'll send money, you know you can't. And you shouldn't act as if it were for four weeks. This business doesn't last a mere four weeks. You

know it and I know it. So don't say, "Well, it's only
for a couple of weeks," as you hand me the fur coat
I won't need till winter. And let's not talk about
misfortune. Let's talk about shame. Oh, Fritz!

*She stops. A door is heard opening. She hastily puts
herself to rights. Her* HUSBAND *comes in.*

HUSBAND: What are you doing, tidying up?

WIFE: No.

HUSBAND: Why are you packing?

WIFE: I want to get away.

HUSBAND: What do you mean?

WIFE: We've talked sometimes about my going away for
a time. Things are not too good here these days.

HUSBAND: That's a lot of nonsense.

WIFE: Shall I stay then?

HUSBAND: Where do you intend to go?

WIFE: To Amsterdam. Away from here.

HUSBAND: But you have no one there.

WIFE: No.

HUSBAND: Why don't you stay here then? You certainly
mustn't go on my account.

WIFE: No.

HUSBAND: You know I've not changed, don't you, Judith?

WIFE: Yes.

*He embraces her. They stand, silent, between the
bags.*

HUSBAND: And there's nothing else to make you go?

WIFE: You know the answer to that.

HUSBAND: Perhaps it isn't so stupid. You need a breather. It's stifling here. I'll bring you back. Two days on the other side of the frontier, and I'd feel much better.

WIFE: Yes, by all means.

HUSBAND: This business here can't last too long. A complete change will come — from somewhere. All this will calm down again like an inflammation. It's really a misfortune.

WIFE: It certainly is. Did you meet Shoeck?

HUSBAND: Yes, that is, only on the stairs. I believe he's sorry now they cut us. He was quite embarrassed. In the long run they can't hold us intellectuals down like this, however much they hate us. Nor can they make war with completely spineless wrecks. These people are not so unresponsive if one confronts them boldly. When do you want to leave?

WIFE: Quarter past nine.

HUSBAND: And where shall I send the money?

WIFE: General Delivery, Amsterdam, perhaps.

HUSBAND: I'll get myself a special permit. My God, I can't send my wife away with ten marks a month! What a mess it all is. I feel awful about it.

WIFE: When you come for me, it'll do you good.

HUSBAND: To see a paper for once that has something in it!

WIFE: I called Gertrude. She'll look after you.

HUSBAND: Quite unnecessary — for a couple of weeks.

WIFE (*she has begun to pack*): Hand me the fur coat now, will you?

HUSBAND (*he gives it to her*): After all, it's only for a couple of weeks.

IN SEARCH OF JUSTICE

CHARACTERS

Judge A

Inspector

Prosecutor

Attendant

Maid

Judge B

The haze of a January morning is seen through the window. A round gas lamp is still burning. JUDGE A *is just putting on his robe. There is a knock at the door.*

JUDGE A: Come in.

A police INSPECTOR *comes in.*

INSPECTOR: Good morning, Judge.

JUDGE A: Good morning, Herr Tallinger. I asked you to come and see me about the case Haeberle, Schuent, and Gaunitzer. I frankly admit the matter is not entirely clear to me.

The INSPECTOR *does not answer.*

I gather from the records that the scene of the affair was Arndt's jewelry store. Arndt is Jewish, isn't he?

Again the INSPECTOR *does not answer.*

And Haeberle, Schuent, and Gaunitzer are still members of Storm Troop Seven in the S.A.? *

The INSPECTOR *nods.*

Which means that the S.A. have seen no need to discipline these three men on their own account?

The INSPECTOR *shakes his head.*

In view of the sensation the affair has created in the neighborhood one can assume that the S.A. has held an investigation?

The INSPECTOR *shrugs his shoulders.*

---

* *Sturm Abteilung, i.e.,* Storm Troop.

I'd be grateful, Tallinger, if you could give me a summary of the whole business before the trial. Can you do that now?

INSPECTOR (*speaking mechanically*): Last year on the second of December at quarter past eight in the morning, three S.A. men, Haeberle, Schuent, and Gaunitzer, broke into Arndt's jewelry store in Sletov Street, exchanged a few words, and wounded Arndt, who is fifty-four years old, on the back of his head. It involved also material damages in the region of 11,834 marks. Police investigations made on December 7 of last year revealed . . .

JUDGE A: My dear Tallinger, that's all in the records. (*Annoyed, he points to the indictment which consists of a single sheet of paper:*) The indictment is the thinnest and sloppiest I've ever seen in my life, and I haven't been spoiled in the last few months either. Nevertheless, all that's in it. I hoped you might be in a position to explain something of the background of the case.

INSPECTOR: Certainly, Your Honor.

JUDGE A: Well?

INSPECTOR: There's no background to the case at all, Your Honor.

JUDGE A: Tallinger, are you really going to maintain that this case is quite straightforward?

INSPECTOR (*grinning*): Why no, of course not.

JUDGE A: It's said that some jewelry got lost during the incident. Has it been recovered since?

INSPECTOR: Not that I know of.

The JUDGE *looks hard at the* INSPECTOR.

I have a family, Your Honor.

JUDGE A: So have I, Tallinger.

INSPECTOR: Yes.

There is a pause.

Arndt is a Jew, don't you see?

JUDGE A: As the name indicates.

INSPECTOR: Right. And there's a rumor going round in the neighborhood. A case of racial pollution.

The JUDGE *appears to begin to understand.*

JUDGE A: Aha. Who was involved?

INSPECTOR: Arndt's daughter. Nineteen. Supposed to be pretty.

JUDGE A: Has the matter been officially gone into?

INSPECTOR (*reluctantly*): Not exactly. The rumor died out again.

JUDGE A: Who spread it then?

INSPECTOR: The owner of the building. A Herr von Miel.

JUDGE A: He wanted to get the Jewish store out of his building?

INSPECTOR: So we thought. But then apparently he went back on it.

JUDGE A: But anyway this would explain why there was some ill feeling against Arndt in the neighborhood? And the young fellows acted out of a sort of patriotic excitement.

INSPECTOR (*he answers with decision*): I don't think so, Your Honor.

JUDGE A: What don't you think?

INSPECTOR: That Haeberle, Schuent, and Gaunitzer will make much of this pollution business.

JUDGE A: Why not?

INSPECTOR: The name of the Aryan concerned was never mentioned in the records. God knows who he is. He could be wherever there's a crowd of Aryans, couldn't he? Well, and where are there crowds of Aryans? In short, the S.A. doesn't want it brought into the discussion.

JUDGE A (*impatiently*): Then why do you tell me?

INSPECTOR: Because you said you had a family. So that *you* won't bring it into the discussion. All the same, some witness from that part of town might start in.

JUDGE A: I understand. But aside from this I don't understand very much.

INSPECTOR: Between ourselves: the less you understand the better.

JUDGE A: It's easy for you to talk. But I have to render a verdict.

INSPECTOR (*vaguely*): Well, yes.

JUDGE A: The only other possibility is direct provocation of the three S.A. men by Arndt himself. Otherwise the episode cannot be explained.

INSPECTOR: Just what *I* think, Your Honor.

JUDGE A: In that case how were the S.A. men provoked?

INSPECTOR: According to their own deposition they were provoked both by Arndt himself and by an unemployed laborer who shoveled snow for Arndt. Evidently they were going to have a drink and as they passed the store, Wagner, the laborer, and Arndt himself called them names.

JUDGE A: But you haven't got a witness for that, have you?

INSPECTOR: Yes. The owner of the house, this Herr von Miel, declared that he saw Wagner provoke the S.A.

men. He saw it through his window. And Arndt's partner, one Herr Stau, visited S.A. headquarters the same afternoon and in the presence of Haeberle, Schuent, and Gaunitzer admitted that Arndt had always spoken contemptuously of the S.A.

JUDGE A: So Arndt has a partner? Aryan?

INSPECTOR: Obviously. Do you think he'd choose a Jew to represent him?

JUDGE A: But then his partner wouldn't make a statement against him?

INSPECTOR (*cunningly*): I'm not so sure.

JUDGE A (*irritated*): What do you mean? The store can't sue for damages if it's proved that Arndt provoked the attack of Haeberle, Schuent, and Gaunitzer.

INSPECTOR: How do you know Stau has any interest in damages?

JUDGE A: I don't understand. He's a partner, isn't he?

INSPECTOR: Exactly.

The JUDGE *looks puzzled.*

We have established that Stau comes and goes at S.A. headquarters — not officially, I mean, but *sub rosa* — and that's probably why Arndt made him his partner. Stau was once involved in a strange affair: the S.A. took someone for a ride but it turned out to be the wrong man, and it was quite a job to fix everything up afterward. Of course I wouldn't go so far as to say that Stau himself in the present case . . . Anyway, you may have to be careful with him. You spoke just now about your family: I know I can trust you to keep this confidential.

JUDGE A (*shaking his head*): What I don't see is this.

How can it be to the interest of Herr Stau that the store should lose over eleven thousand marks?

INSPECTOR: Yes, the jewelry is certainly gone. I mean Haeberle, Schuent, and Gaunitzer don't have it anyway. And they haven't sold it either.

JUDGE A: I see.

INSPECTOR: Naturally Stau can't be expected to keep Arndt on as a partner after Arndt has been found guilty of provocation. As for the losses Arndt has incurred, he'll have to make them good to Stau. Is that clear?

JUDGE A: Certainly that is quite clear.

Thoughtfully, he looks at the INSPECTOR *for a moment. The* INSPECTOR *looks straight in front of him, expressionless and entirely official.*

Yes, and it will boil down to this: Arndt provoked the S.A. men. Apparently he has made himself unpopular everywhere. Didn't you say he gave the owner of the building cause for complaint through the scandalous goings-on of his family? Yes, yes, I know the affair must not be brought into the discussion, but one can readily imagine he won't mind if someone moves out in the near future. Thanks very much, Tallinger. You've done me a real service.

JUDGE A *gives the* INSPECTOR *a cigar. The* INSPECTOR *goes out. In the doorway he meets the Junior* PROSECUTOR *who is just coming in.*

PROSECUTOR (*to* JUDGE A): Can I speak to you a minute?

JUDGE A (*he is now peeling an apple for his lunch*): You can.

PROSECUTOR: It concerns the case of Haeberle, Schuent, and Gaunitzer.

JUDGE A (*busy with the apple*): Yes.

PROSECUTOR: The case is rather straightforward as far as . . .

JUDGE A: Yes. To be quite frank, I don't understand why your prosecutor's office has opened proceedings.

PROSECUTOR: But why? The case has attracted attention rather disagreeably in the neighborhood. Even party members wanted an investigation.

JUDGE A: I see it as merely an obvious case of Jewish provocation and nothing else.

PROSECUTOR: Oh nonsense, Goll! Our indictments may be somewhat laconic these days, but they deserve your closer attention, believe me. Don't be so naive: you must learn to see a little farther than your nose. And take care not to make mistakes or before you know it you'll be a country judge in Eastern Pomerania. It's not too cozy there nowadays.

JUDGE A (*he is perplexed, and stops eating the apple*): I don't understand. You don't mean to say you intend to let the Jew Arndt go?

PROSECUTOR (*on his dignity*): And if I do? The man did not intend provocation. You think he can't get justice in a court of the Third Reich because he's a Jew? You're developing extremely strange opinions, Goll.

JUDGE A (*he is annoyed*): I'm developing no opinions. I merely considered that Haeberle, Schuent, and Gaunitzer were acting under provocation.

PROSECUTOR: They were not provoked by Arndt but by the unemployed laborer, what was his name — um — Wagner.

JUDGE A: There's not a word of it in your indictment, my dear Spitz.

PROSECUTOR: Of course not. All the prosecutor's office

heard was that the S.A. men had attacked Arndt. And then we intervened as a matter of duty. But if for example the witness von Miel says in court that Arndt was never on the street during the whole episode but that, on the contrary, it was the laborer — what was his name — er — Wagner who called them names, somehow we have to take that into account.

JUDGE A: Von Miel is going to make a statement of that sort? But he's the owner of the building. He wants to get Arndt out of the place. He won't make a statement in his favor.

PROSECUTOR: What on earth do you have against von Miel? Why shouldn't he tell the truth under oath? Perhaps you don't know that von Miel is not only in the S.S.,* he has highly influential contacts in the Department of Justice? I would advise you to regard him as a respectable citizen, my dear Goll.

JUDGE A: So I do. After all you don't have to respect a man less these days for not wanting a Jewish store in his house.

PROSECUTOR (*magnanimously*): As long as the man pays the rent. . . .

JUDGE A (*diplomatically*): I'm given to understand that he once gave information against Arndt concerning . . .

PROSECUTOR: So you know that. But aren't you wrong in assuming that von Miel was trying to get Arndt out of the building? The more so since the accusation was withdrawn. Wouldn't one rather assume they had come to a somewhat satisfactory understanding? My dear Goll, please don't be so naive.

JUDGE A (*he is now getting really annoyed*): My dear

---

* *Schutz Staffel*, the black-uniformed elite guards.

Spitz, it is not so simple. His own partner whom I expected to protect him wants to indict him, and the owner of the building who indicted him wants to protect him. And we have to reach a decision.

PROSECUTOR: What are we paid for?

JUDGE A: A frightfully involved affair. Care for a Havana?

The PROSECUTOR *takes a Havana and they smoke in silence. Then* JUDGE A *continues, with gloomy reflectiveness.*

But if it is established in court that Arndt was not guilty of provocation he can immediately bring an action for damages against the S.A.

PROSECUTOR: In the first place he can't bring an action against the S.A. but at best only against Haeberle, Schuent, and Gaunitzer, who haven't a penny — unless he were to get his money out of the unemployed laborer — er — what's his name — er — Wagner. (*With emphasis.*) In the second place he will think twice before indicting the S.A. men.

JUDGE A: Where is he at the moment?

PROSECUTOR: In the hospital.

JUDGE A: And Wagner?

PROSECUTOR: In a concentration camp.

JUDGE A (*he is now somewhat at ease again*): Well, well, in view of the circumstances, it's true, Arndt will hardly wish to accuse the S.A. And Wagner will not bank too much on his innocence. But the S.A. will scarcely be content if the Jew gets off scot-free.

PROSECUTOR: But the court will confirm the fact that the S.A. men were provoked. It doesn't matter to them whether it was the Jew or the communist.

JUDGE A (*he is still in doubt*): That's not quite true.

After all, during the argument between Wagner and the S.A. men the jewelry store was damaged. To a certain extent the S.A. is still implicated.

PROSECUTOR: Well, you can't have it every way, and you can't do right by everybody. But your patriotic feelings must tell you, my dear Goll, whom you *should* do right by. I must stress one thing: I'm advised — and the advice comes from the highest circles in the S.A. — that by now somewhat more backbone is expected from German judges.

JUDGE A (*sighing*): In any case it isn't easy to know what *is* just, my dear Spitz. You must admit that.

PROSECUTOR: By all means. But our Minister of Justice made an excellent remark which might give you something to hold on to: "Whatever's useful to the German Folk is just."

JUDGE A (*apathetically*): Yes, of course.

PROSECUTOR: But cheer up. (*He stands up.*) Now you know the background, it shouldn't be hard. See you later, my dear Goll.

He leaves the room. JUDGE A *is very uneasy. He stands for a time at the window. Then, absentmindedly, he thumbs through the records. Finally he rings. An* ATTENDANT *comes in.*

JUDGE A: Please bring Inspector Tallinger in again from the witness room. And don't be obtrusive about it.

The ATTENDANT *leaves. The* INSPECTOR *comes in again.*

Tallinger, it's lucky I didn't take your advice when you told me to regard it as a case of provocation by Arndt. I hear the Herr von Miel is ready to give evidence under oath that it was the laborer Wagner who was guilty of provocation, and not Arndt.

INSPECTOR (*impenetrably*): That's correct, Your Honor.

JUDGE A: "That's correct?" *Now* what do you mean?

INSPECTOR: That Wagner was the one who called names.

JUDGE A: And isn't that true?

INSPECTOR (*he is offended*): Your Honor: whether it's true of not we can't . . .

JUDGE A (*decisively*): Listen a moment, man. You're in a German Court of Justice. Has Wagner confessed or has he not confessed?

INSPECTOR: Your Honor, I wasn't in the concentration camp in person, if that's what you want to know. In the report of the official investigation — Wagner is reported to have kidney trouble — it says he confessed. Only . . .

JUDGE A: Well then, he confessed. What d'you mean by "only"?

INSPECTOR: He's a World War veteran and, in fact, was shot in the neck, and, according to Stau, who, as you know gave evidence as Arndt's partner, is incapable of speaking out loud. That von Miel on the second floor should be able to hear him shouting at the S.A. men is not wholly . . .

JUDGE A: Oh well, it may of course be said you don't need a voice to tell someone to shove it. A simple gesture would do the job. I have gotten the impression throughout that the prosecutor's office wishes to leave a loophole for the S.A. More correctly stated: that is precisely what they wish.

INSPECTOR: Yes, Your Honor.

JUDGE A: What does Arndt say?

INSPECTOR: That he definitely was not there and got the

wound in the head by falling on the stairs. You can't
get anything more out of him.

JUDGE A: The man is probably quite innocent and got
into this accidentally.

INSPECTOR (*he gives it up*): Yes, Your Honor.

JUDGE A: And the S.A. will be satisfied if their own
people get off?

INSPECTOR: Yes, Your Honor.

JUDGE A: Stop saying, "Yes, Your Honor" like a nut-
cracker.

INSPECTOR: Yes, Your Honor.

JUDGE A: What do you wish to imply? Please don't misunderstand me, Tallinger. You should realize that
I am somewhat nervous. I'm quite aware you're a
man of honor, but when you gave me advice you
must surely have had something in mind?

INSPECTOR (*good-naturedly, he pulls himself together*):
Haven't you ever wondered if the Prosecutor isn't
simply after your job and that's why he leads you up
the garden path? Such cases are not uncommon
nowadays. Let's suppose, Your Honor, you certify
that the Jew is innocent. He didn't provoke those
fellows. Wasn't even there. Got that hole in the
back of his head quite accidentally in a fight between
other people. And so after a time he returns to the
store. Stau can't stop him. And the store has been
damaged to the tune of eleven thousand marks. But
now Stau shares the losses since he can't demand
the eleven thousand marks from Arndt. And so Stau,
if I know the type, will apply to the S.A. for com-
pensation for the lost jewels. Naturally he won't go
to them himself since he's the associate of a Jew
and therefore "a lackey of the Jews." But he'll have
other people on hand. Then it'll be said that the

S.A. in its patriotic enthusiasm grabs jewelry! You can imagine what the S.A. will think of your verdict then. The general run of people won't understand it anyway. For in the Third Reich how can a Jew put the S.A. in the wrong?

For some time there has been a noise in the rear. Now it gets rather loud.

JUDGE A: What's that frightful noise? One moment, Tallinger.

He rings and the ATTENDANT *comes in.*

What's all the row about?

ATTENDANT: The courtroom is full. And they're jammed so close together in the aisles no one can get through. And there are some S.A. men who say they have to get through; they're under orders to attend the trial.

The ATTENDANT *leaves, while* JUDGE A *merely looks frightened.*

INSPECTOR (*continuing*): You'll get it in the neck from those people, you know. I strongly advise you to concentrate on Arndt and leave the S.A. in peace.

JUDGE A (*he sits down, brokenly, his head in his hands. He is very tired*): Very good, Tallinger, I'll have to think it over.

INSPECTOR: You'll be well advised to do just that, Your Honor.

He goes out. JUDGE A *stands up with difficulty, and noisily rings the bell. The* ATTENDANT *comes in.*

JUDGE A: Go over to Judge Fey and ask him if he could come over and see me for a few minutes.

The ATTENDANT *leaves.* JUDGE A'*s housemaid comes in with a lunch bag.*

MAID: You'd forget your head, Your Honor. It's really dreadful. Look what you've forgotten today. Think hard for a moment: the main thing! (*She hands the bag over to him.*) Your lunch bag! And then you'd have to buy those warm rolls and you'd get a stomach-ache like last week. All because you don't take care of yourself.

JUDGE A: Very well, Mary.

MAID: I could hardly get through. The whole building is full of S.A. men on account of the trial. But today it's coming to them, isn't it, Your Honor? At the butcher's, people were saying: "It's good there's some justice left in the world." Knocking down a respectable man of business! The whole neighborhood knows half the S.A. are former criminals. Except for the judges and the courts they'd run off with the cathedral. They did it for the rings. One of them — Haeberle — is marrying a girl who was on the streets till six months ago. And they assaulted Wagner, the laborer with a wound in the neck, while he was shoveling snow. Everybody saw it. They do it quite openly. They're terrorizing the whole neighborhood. And if anyone says anything, they wait for him after dark and when they hit him he doesn't get up again.

JUDGE A: Very well, Mary. Now run along.

MAID: I said in the butcher's: "Judge Goll will give them their comeuppance." Am I right? You have the decent people on your side, that's a fact, Your Honor. Only don't eat your lunch too quickly, it's bad for you. It's so unhealthy, and now I'm going. I won't be keeping you any longer. You have to go into court and don't let it excite you or you may as well eat now. You don't need more than a minute or two, and *that* won't make any difference. But you can't eat on an excited stomach. Now take care of yourself. Your health is your most treasured possession. Now I'm going. I can see you're dying to go into court, you know you are, and I must get to the grocery store.

The MAID *leaves.* JUDGE B, *an elderly judge and friend of* JUDGE A, *comes in.*

JUDGE B: What's the matter?

JUDGE A: I wanted to talk something out with you if you have a few minutes to spare. This afternoon I have a rather dreadful case to deal with.

JUDGE B (*he sits down*): Yes, the S.A. affair.

JUDGE A (*he suddenly stands still*): Who told *you?*

JUDGE B: It was discussed over there yesterday afternoon. A nasty case.

JUDGE A *begins to pace up and down.*

JUDGE A: What do they say?

JUDGE B: Nobody envies you. (*Inquisitively.*) What are you going to do?

JUDGE A: I don't know. Moreover, I didn't know the case was so well known.

JUDGE B (*he is surprised*): Really?

JUDGE A: They say this partner is quite a dangerous type.

JUDGE B: He certainly is. But this von Miel is also no philanthropist.

JUDGE A: What is known about him?

JUDGE B: Enough. He has contacts.

There is a pause.

JUDGE A: Highly influential contacts?

JUDGE B: Highly influential.

Another pause.

(*Cautiously.*) If you leave the Jew out of it and acquit Haeberle, Schuent, and Gaunitzer on the grounds that they were provoked by the laborer who then ran back into the store, won't the S.A. be satisfied? In any case Arndt won't bring charges against the S.A.

JUDGE A (*he is troubled*): You forget Arndt's partner. He'll go to the S.A. to claim the valuables. And then I'll have the whole leadership of the S.A. at my throat, Fey.

JUDGE B (*after he has considered this argument, which apparently surprises him*): But if you leave the Jew out of it, von Miel will most certainly break your neck. Perhaps you don't know about the bills of exchange at his bank? He's clutching at Arndt as a drowning man clutches at a straw.

JUDGE A (*he is appalled*): Bills of exchange!

There is a knock at the door.

JUDGE B: Come in.

ATTENDANT: Your Honor, I really don't know how I can reserve seats for the Senior Prosecutor and the President of the District Court. If you gentlemen would only let me know in time!

JUDGE B (*since* JUDGE A *is silent*): Keep two seats free and don't disturb us in here.

The ATTENDANT *leaves.*

JUDGE A: That's the last straw.

JUDGE B: Von Miel cannot in any circumstance abandon Arndt and allow him to be ruined. He needs him.

JUDGE A (*annihilated*): As a milch cow.

JUDGE B: I said nothing of the kind, my dear Goll! I don't understand how you can think it of me! I really don't! I must insist that I said *nothing* against Herr von Miel. I'm sorry this is necessary, Goll.

JUDGE A (*getting excited*): But you can't take it that way, Fey. Remember our relationship!

JUDGE B: What d'you mean "our relationship"? I cannot meddle in your cases. Whether you want to be in with the Minister of Justice or the S.A. you must do it yourself. In these days, after all, *everyone* must look out for himself.

JUDGE A: I *am* looking out for myself! Only I don't know what advice to give myself!

He stands in the doorway listening to the noise outside.

JUDGE B: A bad business.

JUDGE A: My God, I'm willing to do anything, please understand me. You've changed completely. I decide this and I decide that as they require but at least I must know *what* they require. When you don't know that, there's no justice left.

JUDGE B: If I were you, I wouldn't be shouting "there's no justice left," Goll!

JUDGE A: Now what have I said again? I didn't mean that! I only mean . . . if such contradictions exist . . .

JUDGE B: We consider ourselves a "people of brothers."

JUDGE A: Yes, of course. I never said anything different. Please don't weigh every word I say!

JUDGE B: Why not? I'm a judge.

JUDGE A (*sweating*): My dear Fey, if one weighed every word of every judge . . . I am quite willing to examine the whole case in the most rigorous and con-

scientious manner but I *must* be told which decision
is in the interest of the higher authorities. If I let
the Jew stay in the store, I naturally make the owner
of the building angry . . . No, not the owner, I mean
the partner . . . I'm getting hopelessly confused.
And if the laborer was the source of provocation,
the owner — what's his name? — von Miel wants . . .
They can't transfer me to Eastern Pomerania, I have
a rupture, and I want nothing to do with the S.A.
After all I have a family, Fey. It's easy for my wife
to say I should merely find out what really happened: I'd wake up in the hospital. Am I to speak of
an attack? Am I to speak of provocation? What
do they want of me? Naturally I don't sentence the
S.A. but either the Jew or the unemployed laborer.
But which? How am I to choose between the laborer
and the Jew? Between the partner and the land-
lord? In any case I won't go to Pomerania, that's
out of the question, Fey. I'd rather go to a concentration camp. Don't look at me like that: I'm not
the accused. I'm willing to do *anything.*

JUDGE B: Willingness is not everything, my friend. (*He
stands up.*)

JUDGE A: Who is to decide, then?

JUDGE B: In general, a judge's conscience tells him that,
Herr Goll. Remember. Good-bye.

JUDGE A: Yes, of course. "According to his knowledge
and his conscience." But in this case: *what* am I to
choose? What, Fey?

JUDGE B *has left. Speechless,* JUDGE A *stands looking after him. The telephone rings.*

(*He picks up the receiver.*) Yes? — Emmy? —
They can't come to what? The bowling party? Who
called you up? — Attorney Priesnitz? — Who told
him? — What do I mean? I have to pronounce a
verdict.

He hangs up. The ATTENDANT *comes in. The noise of the crowd is loud again.*

ATTENDANT: Haeberle, Schuent, and Gaunitzer, Your Honor.

JUDGE A (*gathering up his documents*): Coming.

ATTENDANT: I found a seat for the President of the District Court at the press table. He was quite satisfied. But the Senior Prosecutor refused to sit at the judge's table. For then you'd have to conduct the trial from the dock, Your Honor. (*He laughs absurdly at his joke.*)

JUDGE A: I won't do that in any circumstances!

ATTENDANT: Here's the door, Your Honor. Where did you put your brief case with the indictment in it?

JUDGE A (*absolutely bewildered*): Yes, that's what I want. Or else I won't know who is accused, will I? What shall we do with the Senior Prosecutor?

ATTENDANT: Now you've put your address book under your arm, Your Honor. Here's your brief case. (*He stuffs it under the Judge's arms.*)

Distracted and wiping the sweat from his brow, JUDGE A *goes into the court.*

THE INFORMER

CHARACTERS

Husband

Wife

Boy

Maid

It is a rainy Sunday afternoon. Father, mother, and child have just finished lunch. MAID *enters.*

MAID: Herr and Frau Klimbtsch want to know if you're at home, sir.

HUSBAND (*snapping*): We're not.

The MAID *goes out.*

WIFE: You should have gone to the phone yourself. They know we couldn't possibly have gone out yet.

HUSBAND: Why couldn't we have gone out?

WIFE: Because it's raining.

HUSBAND: That's not a reason.

WIFE: What would we have gone out for? They'll certainly wonder about that now.

HUSBAND: There are plenty of places to go to.

WIFE: Then why don't we go?

HUSBAND: Where should we go to?

WIFE: If only it weren't raining.

HUSBAND: And where on earth should we go if it weren't raining?

WIFE: In the old days you could at least arrange to meet somebody.

There is a pause.

It was a mistake not to go to the phone. Now they know we don't want them here.

HUSBAND: What if they do?

WIFE: Why, then it means we're dropping them just when everybody's dropping them. I don't like it.

HUSBAND: We're not dropping them.

WIFE: Then why shouldn't they come here?

HUSBAND: Because this Klimbtsch fellow bores me stiff.

WIFE: In the old days he didn't bore you.

HUSBAND: "In the old days!" Don't keep saying that. You make me nervous.

WIFE: At any rate you wouldn't have cut him in the old days just because his case is being looked into by the school inspectors.

HUSBAND: Are you suggesting I'm a coward?

There is a pause.

All right. Call them and say we've just come back because of the rain.

The WIFE *remains seated.*

WIFE: Shall we ask the Lemkes if they want to come over?

HUSBAND: So they can tell us we're not keen enough on Civil Defense?

WIFE (*to the* BOY): Klaus-Heinrich! Leave the radio alone.

The BOY *turns to the newspapers.*

HUSBAND: It's certainly a catastrophe to have rain today. You just can't live in a country where it's a catastrophe when it rains.

WIFE: Is it wise to throw remarks like that around?

HUSBAND: Within my own four walls I can make whatever remarks I please. In my own home I can say what I . . .

He is interrupted. The MAID *comes in with the coffee things. There is silence while she is in the room.*

Must we have a maid whose father is Block Warden?*

WIFE: I think we've talked about that enough. Last time you said it had its advantages.

HUSBAND: I've said a lot of things. Only say something of the sort to your mother and we'll be in a wonderful mess.

WIFE: What I say to my mother . . . !

The MAID *interrupts them again as she brings in the coffee.*

Leave it now, Erna, you can go. I'll look after this.

MAID: Thanks very much, Madame. (*She goes out.*)

BOY (*looking up from the paper*): Do all priests do this, Papa?

HUSBAND: What?

BOY: What it says here.

HUSBAND: What is it you're reading? (*He snatches the paper out of his hand.*)

BOY: Our Group Leader told us we could all know what it says in *this* paper.

HUSBAND: I don't care what the Group Leader said. I decide what you can read and what you can't.

WIFE: Here's ten cents, Klaus-Heinrich, go buy yourself something.

BOY: But it's raining. (*He hangs around near the window, undecided.*)

---

* — and therefore a Nazi.

HUSBAND: If these reports of the priest trials don't stop, I won't order this paper any more.

WIFE: And which one *will* you subscribe to? It's in all of them.

HUSBAND: If all the papers carry filth like that, I'll read none. I couldn't know less of what's going on in the world.

WIFE: A house cleaning doesn't hurt once in a while.

HUSBAND: House cleaning! That's just politics.

WIFE: Anyway it's no concern of ours: we're Lutherans.

HUSBAND: It's not a matter of indifference for our people if they can't think of a church without also thinking of such abominations.

WIFE: Then what should they do if such things happen?

HUSBAND: What should they do? Maybe they might look to their own affairs. It may not all be as clean as it might be in their own Brown House, so I hear.

WIFE: But that goes to prove our people has recovered its health, Karl.

HUSBAND: If that's what health looks like, give me disease.

WIFE: You're nervous today. Did anything happen at school?

HUSBAND: What should happen at school? And please stop telling me I'm nervous. That's what makes me so.

WIFE: We shouldn't always be quarreling, Karl. In the old days . . .

HUSBAND: I was waiting for it: "in the old days!" I didn't want my child's mind poisoned in the old days and I don't want it poisoned now!

WIFE: Where is he anyway?

HUSBAND: How do I know?

WIFE: Did you see him leave?

HUSBAND: No.

WIFE: I don't understand where he can have gone. (*Shouting.*) Klaus-Heinrich!

She runs out and is heard shouting. She returns.

Well, he's out.

HUSBAND: Why on earth shouldn't he be out?

WIFE: Why, because it's simply pouring.

HUSBAND: Why are you so nervous if the boy goes out once in a while?

WIFE: What have you been saying?

HUSBAND: What's that got to do with it?

WIFE: You're so uncontrolled these days.

HUSBAND: I certainly am not uncontrolled these days, but, even if I were, what has that got to do with the boy being out?

WIFE: Oh, you know they listen.

HUSBAND: So what?

WIFE: So what? What if he tells tales? You know what's drummed into them at the Hitler Youth. They're under orders to report *everything*. Strange he left so quietly.

HUSBAND: Nonsense!

WIFE: Didn't you notice it, when he'd left?

HUSBAND: He was at the window quite a while.

WIFE: I wonder what he overheard.

HUSBAND: He knows what happens to people who get denounced.

WIFE: What of the boy the Schmulkes told about? His father must be in the concentration camp still. If only we knew how long he was in the room.

HUSBAND: Oh, that's all nonsense.

He goes through the other room and shouts for the BOY.

WIFE: I can't believe he'd just go off without saying a word. He isn't like that.

HUSBAND: Maybe he's at some school friend's.

WIFE: In that case he can only be at the Mummermann's. I'll phone. (*She phones.*)

HUSBAND: I regard the whole thing as a false alarm.

WIFE (*at the phone*): This is Frau Studienrat* Furcke. Good afternoon, Frau Mummermann. Is Klaus-Heinrich at your place? — He isn't? — Then I just can't think where the boy is. — Tell me, Frau Mummermann, is the club room of the Hitler Youth open Sunday afternoon? — It is? — Thanks, I'll try them.

She hangs up. The couple sit in silence.

HUSBAND: What can he have heard after all?

WIFE: You talked about the paper. You shouldn't have said that about the Brown House. He's such a nationalist.

HUSBAND: And *what* may I have said about the Brown House?

WIFE: You can hardly have forgotten: that it's not clean!

---

* Title of a teacher's wife.

HUSBAND: That can't be interpreted as an attack. To say: it's not clean, or rather as I more moderately put it, not *quite* clean, which certainly makes a difference, a considerable difference, why, that's more of a jocular observation, idiomatic and popular, one might almost say a colloquialism. It means little more than that probably, even there, something is not always, and under all circumstances, as the Führer wishes it. I intentionally indicated the merely probable character of my allegation by using the expression: "it *may* not all be *quite*" — *quite* in the mildest sense — "clean." This was my formulation of the matter. *May* be! Not: *is!* I can't say that anything there *is* not clean, there's no proof. But wherever there are men, there are imperfections. I never suggested anything more than that, and that only in the mildest form. The Führer himself on a certain occasion said much the same thing a good deal more sharply!

WIFE: I don't understand. You don't have to talk this way to me.

HUSBAND: I wish I didn't. I'm not sure what you yourself say, in the way of gossip, about the things you've heard between these four walls, insignificant things, probably only said in a moment of excitement. Naturally I'm far from accusing you of spreading frivolous tales against your husband and I don't for a moment assume the boy would do anything against his father. But unfortunately there is an important distinction between *doing* wrong and *knowing* you do it.

WIFE: Now please stop! Watch *your* tongue! You said one can't live in Hitler Germany. All along I've been trying to remember whether you said that before or after what you said about the Brown House.

HUSBAND: I didn't say it at all.

WIFE: You go on as if I were the police! What can the boy have heard? That's what tortures me.

HUSBAND: The expression "Hitler Germany" is not in my vocabulary.

WIFE: And about the Block Warden and about the papers being full of lies and what you said recently about Civil Defense — the boy hears nothing positive at all! That certainly isn't good for a young mind. Youth can only be perverted by such talk. The Führer always stresses: "Germany's youth is Germany's future." The boy doesn't run off and turn informer. He isn't made that way. I feel bad.

HUSBAND: He's revengeful.

WIFE: What can he take revenge *for?*

HUSBAND: God knows. There's always something. Maybe because I took his green frog away from him.

WIFE: That was a week ago.

HUSBAND: He remembers.

WIFE: Why did you take it?

HUSBAND: Because he caught no flies for it. Just let it starve.

WIFE: He really has too much to do, though.

HUSBAND: That's not the frog's fault!

WIFE: But he never said anything about that. And just now I gave him ten cents. Why, he gets everything he wants.

HUSBAND: Bribery!

WIFE: What do you mean?

HUSBAND: They'll say we tried to bribe him to keep his mouth shut.

WIFE: What do you think they can do to you?

HUSBAND: Oh, everything. There are no limits to what they can do. Good God! "Educator of the youth!" I fear them. To be a teacher in such circumstances!

WIFE: But there's nothing against you.

HUSBAND: There's something against everyone. All are suspect. If suspicion exists, one is suspected. Suspicion need only exist.

WIFE: A child is not a reliable witness. A child has no idea what he's saying.

HUSBAND: That's *your* opinion. Since when have *they* needed a witness for anything?

WIFE: Can't we figure out what you must have meant by your remarks? I mean: then it will be clear he misunderstood.

HUSBAND: What could I have said? I can't remember. It's the fault of the damned rain. . . . It makes you disgruntled. After all I'd be the last to say anything against the spiritual revival the German people have experienced! I saw it coming in 1932.

WIFE: Karl, we haven't time to talk. We must straighten everything out at once. We haven't a moment to lose.

HUSBAND: I can't think it of Klaus-Heinrich.

WIFE: Now: first this matter of the Brown House and the filth.

HUSBAND: I said nothing about filth.

WIFE: You said the paper is full of filth and you intend to cancel your subscription.

HUSBAND: Yes, the paper, not the Brown House.

WIFE: Mightn't you have said you disapprove of such filth in the churches? And you think it's quite possible the very men now on trial invented the atrocity stories about the Brown House and *they* said that it wasn't clean? Therefore, *they* should have looked to their own affairs? Above all, you told the boy to leave the radio and read the paper instead because you take the stand that youth in the Third Reich should note with open eyes what is going on?

HUSBAND: All this wouldn't help in the least.

WIFE: Karl, don't let your courage fail you. You must be strong, as the Führer always . . .

HUSBAND: I can't stand in the dock with my own flesh and blood in the witness stand giving evidence against me!

WIFE: You mustn't take it this way.

HUSBAND: It is unpardonably careless to have anything to do with the Klimbtsches!

WIFE: Why? Nothing's happened to him yet.

HUSBAND: But an investigation is pending.

WIFE: An investigation is pending for a lot of people. What would happen if they were all in despair?

HUSBAND: Do you think the Block Warden has anything against us?

WIFE: You mean if inquiries are made? He got a box of cigarettes on his birthday and a splendid tip at New Year's.

HUSBAND: The Gauffs next door gave *fifteen* marks!

WIFE: They read Vorwärts as late as '32 and in May '33 they put out the black-white-and-red flag.*

The telephone rings.

HUSBAND: The telephone!

WIFE: Shall I go?

HUSBAND: I don't know.

WIFE: Who can it be?

HUSBAND: Wait a while. If it rings again, you can answer it.

They wait. It does not ring again.

This isn't living.

WIFE: Karl!

HUSBAND: You bore me a Judas. He sits at the table listening while he drinks the soup we place before him! He commits to memory the conversation of his own parents! He's an informer!

WIFE: You mustn't say that!

There is a pause.

Do you think we should make preparations?

HUSBAND: Do you think they'll come with him *now*?

WIFE: It's quite impossible.

HUSBAND: Maybe I should put on my Iron Cross?

WIFE: By all means, Karl.

He brings the cross and puts it on with trembling fingers.

There's nothing against you at school?

---

* The references are to the organ of the Social Democrats and the colors of the Nationalists.

HUSBAND: How should I know? I'm willing to teach
everything they want taught. But what *do* they want
taught? If only I ever knew! How do I know *how*
they want Bismarck to have been if they're so slow
bringing out the new textbooks? Can't you give the
maid another ten marks? *She's* always listening too.

WIFE (*nods*): And the picture of Hitler. Shall we hang
it over your desk? It'll look better.

HUSBAND: Yes, do that.

The WIFE *begins to move the pictures.*

But if the boy says we hung it specially, it'll all end
in "consciousness of guilt."

She puts the picture back where it was.

Wasn't that the door?

WIFE: I heard nothing.

HUSBAND: There!

WIFE: Karl! (*She throws her arms around him.*)

HUSBAND: Don't lose your nerve. Pack me some underwear.

The door is heard opening. HUSBAND *and* WIFE *stand
close together, petrified, in the corner of the room.
The door opens and in comes the* BOY, *a bag of
chocolates in his hand. There is a silence.*

BOY: What's the matter?

WIFE: Where've you been?

The BOY *points to the bag of chocolates.*

Have you only been buying chocolate?

BOY: Sure. What do you think?

He walks, munching, across the room and out. His parents look after him searchingly.

HUSBAND: Do you think he's telling the truth?

The WIFE *shrugs her shoulders.*

THE ELEPHANT CALF

or

The provability of any and every contention

CHARACTERS

Polly Baker

Uriah Shelley

Jesse Mahoney

Galy Gay (Jeraiah Jip)

Soldiers

> NOTE: In *A Man's A Man*, Galy Gay has turned into Jeraiah Jip. In the present play, he is called Galy Gay by the author, Jeraiah Jip by his comrades.

Theatre: a platform beneath a few rubber trees. Chairs in front of it. This "theatre" is seen from the side, we see both behind and in front of the curtain.

POLLY (*in front of the curtain*): So that dramatic art can have its full effect on you, you are requested to smoke to your heart's content. Our artists are the best in the world, the drinks are one hundred percent, the chairs are comfortable, bets will be taken at the bar on how the plot comes out, and the act curtain will fall each time the audience bets. And please don't shoot the piano player, he's doing his best. Whoever can't immediately understand the plot needn't fret, it is incomprehensible. If all you want to see is something that makes sense, go to the urinal. Your money isn't returnable in any case. This is our comrade Jip who has the honor of playing Pal Jacky the elephant calf. If you consider it too hard a job, my answer is: a theatrical artist must be able to do everything.

SOLDIER (*out front*): Bravo!

POLLY: Jesse Mahoney here will play Pal Jacky's mother, and Uriah Shelley, connoisseur of international horse racing, will play the Moon. You will also have the pleasure of seeing me, Polly Baker, in the featured role of the Banana Tree.

SOLDIERS: Get going. And remember: ten cents for such junk is highway robbery.

POLLY: We are not going to let ourselves be influenced by such vulgar aspersions. The play deals, in the main, with a crime this elephant calf committed. I tell you this so we needn't keep interrupting.

URIAH (*behind the curtain*): Allegedly committed.

59

POLLY: Quite right. That's what comes of studying only my own role. Actually, the elephant calf is innocent.

SOLDIERS (*in rhythm*): Get going! Get going! Get going!

POLLY: One moment (*Steps behind the curtain.*) I fear we may have charged too much for admission, what do you say?

URIAH: This is hardly the moment to think of such things. This is the time to take the plunge!

POLLY: It's just that the play is so weak. You probably don't quite recall, Jesse, what it was like when we did it in the regular theatre. And the parts you've forgotten, Jesse, were the main things, I believe. Wait. Just a minute. I want to go to the bathroom.

Curtain up.

I am the Banana Tree.

SOLDIER: At long last!

POLLY: The Banana Tree: Judge of the Jungle. Here I stand, on the parched plateau of the southern Punjab — as I have done since the invention of elephants. Sometimes, mostly of an evening, the Moon comes up to me, bringing charges — against an elephant calf, for example.

URIAH: Not so fast. That's half the play. For ten cents!

(*He — i.e., the Moon — rises.*)

POLLY: Oh, Moon, hello! Where are you coming from so late in the evening?

URIAH: I've been hearing quite a story about an elephant calf —

POLLY: You're bringing charges against it?

URIAH: Well, naturally.

POLLY: So the elephant calf's committed a crime?

URIAH: Right! You have guessed, and you have guessed right! Effective proof of your perspicuity! Nothing escapes you!

POLLY: Think nothing of it. The elephant calf has murdered its mother, hasn't it?

URIAH: It has, yes.

POLLY: And that's terrible.

URIAH: It's frightful.

POLLY: If only I hadn't mislaid my horn-rimmed glasses!

URIAH: Oh, I have a pair here, as it happens, maybe they're right for you.

POLLY: They'd certainly be right if they also had lenses in them but they have no lenses in them.

URIAH: Still, they're better than nothing.

POLLY: Where's the laugh on that line?

URIAH: Yes, I wonder. So I'll bring these charges against the Moon. I mean: against the elephant calf.

PAL JACKY *comes slowly on.*

POLLY: Ah, yes, here's the nice little elephant calf. Where are you coming from, hm?

GALY GAY: I'm the elephant calf. Seven Rajahs presided at my cradle. What are you laughing at, Moon?

URIAH: Just go right on talking, Elephant.

GALY GAY: My name is Pal Jacky. I'm taking a walk.

POLLY: So you've smashed your mother to bits, have you?

GALY GAY: I smashed her milk jars to bits.

URIAH: And it cracked her skull, eh?

GALY GAY: No, Moon, it fell on a stone.

POLLY: But you did do it, as sure as I'm a Banana Tree?

URIAH: And as sure as I'm the Moon, I'll prove it. My first proof is this lady here.

JESSE *comes on as* PAL JACKY's *mother.*

POLLY: Who's this?

URIAH: The mother.

POLLY: Yes. Remarkable when you come to think of it.

URIAH: Not at all.

POLLY: I find it bizarre — that she's here, I mean.

URIAH: I don't.

POLLY: Then she can stay. Only: it must be proved. Naturally.

URIAH: Yes. You're the judge.

POLLY: Yes. Well then, Elephant Calf, prove you didn't murder your mother.

SOLDIER (*out front*): And with her standing there!

URIAH (*to him*): That's just it, though.

SOLDIER: Even the beginning is lousy. With the mother standing there! This play has no further interest for me.

JESSE: I am this elephant calf's mother. I'll take a bet my little Jacky can prove he's not a murderer. Can't you, Jacky pal?

URIAH: And I'll take a bet he can never in this world prove it.

POLLY (*roaring*): Curtain!

The audience goes silently to the bar, then orders cocktails in loud, clamorous voices.

POLLY (*behind the curtain*): Went pretty nicely. No cat-calls at all.

GALY GAY: But why did no one clap?

JESSE: Maybe they're enthralled.

POLLY: It's so interesting, you see.

URIAH: If we could only show them the thighs of a few chorus girls, they'd trample these benches under foot. Go out on stage. We must try the betting.

POLLY (*comes out*): Gentlemen —

SOLDIERS: Cut it out. The intermission's too short. First let us drink: we need to — in the circumstances.

POLLY: We just wondered if maybe you wouldn't like to take bets. I mean on each side. Mother versus Moon.

SOLDIERS: The gall of the man. So that's how they'll get more money out of us. Well, let's wait till this thing gets moving. The beginning is never any good.

POLLY: All right. Whoever wants to back the Mother, this way. (*Nobody comes forward.*) Those who're for the Moon, this way.

Nobody comes forward, POLLY *goes off, very upset.*

URIAH (*behind the curtain*): Did they bet?

POLLY: Not specially. They think the best is yet to come. That upsets me.

JESSE: They're drinking desperately. It's as if they couldn't bear to go on listening.

URIAH: We'll have to try music. It'll cheer them up.

POLLY (*comes on*): From now on, phonograph music!
Curtain up.

Step this way, Moon, Mother, and Elephant, and you shall forthwith see this enigmatic crime completely cleared up. (*To the audience:*) So will you. How do you intend to conceal the fact anyway that you, Pal Jacky, stabbed your worthy mother to death?

GALY GAY: How *can* I have done so? Being but a girl, and frail?

POLLY: Oh, I see. Well then, I contend that you, Pal Jacky, are not a girl as you claim. Just listen to my first great proof. I remember a bizarre story from my childhood in Whitechapel —

SOLDIER: The Southern Punjab!

Ringing laughter.

POLLY: — Southern Punjab. There was this man who put on a girl's skirt so he wouldn't have to go to war. The sergeant came along with a bullet which he threw in his lap and because he didn't spread his legs out, as girls do, to catch the bullet in his skirt, the sergeant knew it was a man, as in this case. (*They enact this.*) So. You have all seen that the elephant calf is a man. Curtain!

Curtain. Feeble applause.

POLLY: We have a hit on our hands, just listen. Get that curtain up. Curtain call!

They bow. Curtain. No applause.

URIAH: They're loaded with hostility. We can't win.

JESSE: We'll just have to stop, and give them their money back. To be lynched or not to be lynched, that is the question, that's how horribly far things have gone. Just look out front!

URIAH: Give 'em their money back? Never! No theatre in the world can afford *that!*

SOLDIERS: Tomorrow: forward to Tibet! You know, Georgie, these may be the last rubber trees you'll ever drink four-cent cocktails under! The weather isn't pleasant enough for a war, or it'd be nice to stay right here — only it's up north that the game's to be played!

SOLDIER: Anyhow why not let loose with a little song, such as: "Wipe your jackboots, Johnny"?

SOLDIERS: Great! (*They sing:*) "Wipe your . . ."

URIAH: They're singing on their own now. We must proceed!

POLLY: I wish I was in the auditorium. That Johnny thing is a lovely song. If only *we* had thought of something like that. Let's get going.

Curtain up.

After . . . (*He combats the song.*) Now that the elephant calf —

SOLDIER: Still that elephant calf!

POLLY: I said, now that the elephant —

SOLDIER: Calf!

POLLY: Now that . . . a certain animal has been unmasked by my first great proof as a swindler, there comes my second, and still greater, proof.

SOLDIER: Can't you leave this one out, Polly?

URIAH: Yeah, Polly, just you dare.

POLLY: I'm contending that you are a murderer, Pal Jacky. So prove to me that you cannot murder — the Moon, for instance.

SOLDIER: But this is all wrong. The Banana Tree must prove that.

POLLY: Precisely. Just watch. This is a specially exciting point in the drama. "You must prove," I was saying, "that you could never murder — the Moon, for instance. So climb up this clinging creeper here and bring your knife with you."

GALY GAY *does so. The creeper is a rope-ladder which the Moon holds above him.*

SOLDIER (*getting a few who want to go on singing to be quiet*): Quiet! It's not so easy to climb up that thing, he can't see out of that elephant's head!

JESSE: This has *got* to work! Now, Uriah, a voice of thunder!

URIAH *lets out a cry.*

POLLY: What's the matter, Moon? Why the shouting?

URIAH: Because it hurts like crazy! This must definitely be a murderer who's coming up to me!

GALY GAY: Hang this rope-ladder on a bough, Uriah! I am very heavy.

URIAH: Oh! it's tearing my hand off! My hand! My hand! It's tearing my hand off!

POLLY: Just look! Look!

GALY GAY *has* URIAH's *— artificial — hand in his hand; he exhibits it.*

JESSE: That's bad, Jacky. I wouldn't have thought it of you. You're not my child.

URIAH (*holding up his stump*): I testify that he is a murderer!

POLLY: Now all take a look at the bloody stump with which he testifies that you, Pal Jacky, have not proved that you cannot commit murder, for you have so dealt with the Moon that he will certainly bleed to death by morning. Curtain!

Curtain. He steps out.

Now if there are any bets — go to the bar!

SOLDIERS (*go to bet*): One cent on the Moon. Half a cent on the elephant.

URIAH: They bite, you see! You'd have them eating out of your hand, Jesse, if you did your Monologue of a Mother's Grief.

Curtain up.

JESSE:
Of all our earthly or unearthly joys
There's nothing like a mother — is there, boys?
A mother's heart has fed you with her blood.
A mother's hand has given you your food.
A mother's eye has shielded you from wrath.
A mother's foot has kicked the stones from your path.

Laughter.

When mother's body goes beneath the sod
A noble soul flies, lickety-split, to God.

Laughter.

Hear now a mother cry in her great woe:
"To think this beast was once my embryo!"

Big, long laughter.

SOLDIERS: Encore! Worth the price of admission — all ten cents of it! Great! Hurrah! Three cheers for Mother! Hip, hip, hurray!

The curtain falls.

URIAH: Get cracking. This is success. On stage!

Curtain up.

POLLY: I have proved that you are a man who can commit murder. Now I have a question for you, Jacky. Do you contend that this is your mother?

SOLDIERS: Damned unjust, this business, it goes against the grain. But it's philosophical, all right. They're bound to have some kind of happy ending ready, we can depend on that. Quiet!

POLLY: Naturally I wouldn't contend that any son of woman would touch a hair of his very own Mummy-wummy, not in territory governed by old England.

Bravos.

Rule Britannia!

All sing: "Rule Britannia."

Thank you, gentlemen. So long as that soul-shaking song issues from rough, manly throats all is well with old England. To proceed. Since, O Pal Jacky, you have murdered this universally loved lady, this truly great artist,

Bravos.

it obviously cannot be the case, can it, Jacky, old man, that you are the son — or daughter — of the said distinguished lady?

Bravos.

No. What a banana tree contends he can also prove.

Applause.

Therefore, O Moon of Cooch Behar, take a piece of billiard chalk and draw a good solid circle right on the middle of this stage. Then take a plain ordinary piece of rope in your hand and wait till this mother — stricken to the very heart, as she is — steps into the circle which you have now finished drawing, if rather badly. Place this rope — with care — about her snow-white neck.

SOLDIER: Her lovely snow-white neck, her lovely snow-white neck!

POLLY: Quite right. But you — the alleged Pal Jacky — take the other end of this rope of justice and stand outside the circle opposite the Moon. Right. Now, woman, I put a question to you: Have you given birth to a murderer? No answer? Well then, I only wanted to show you, gentlemen, that the very Mother, whom you now see before you, turns away from her fallen child. But in a minute I'll show you even more than that. For now the fearful sun of justice will shine into the secret depths.

SOLDIERS: Now, Polly, don't go too far! Psst!

POLLY: Pal Jacky, for the last time: do you still contend that you are the son of this unhappy creature here?

GALY GAY: Yes.

POLLY: I see. I see. So you're her son, eh? Not long ago you would have it you were her daughter. But then you don't aim at one hundred percent accuracy, do you? We go on now to the principal proof, the first and last and all-embracing proof, a proof which will satisfy you all, gentlemen. If, Jacky, you are the child of this mother, then the strength will be given to you to pull her out of the circle on that side. So much is clear.

SOLDIERS: Crystal clear. Clear as *cracked* crystal. Stop. This is all wrong. Jacky: stand by the truth!

POLLY: I shall count three. One. Two. Three.

GALY GAY *pulls* JESSE *out of the circle.*

JESSE: Hey! Stop! God damn it! What are you up to! Ouch, my neck!

SOLDIERS: Neck, neck? Pull, Jacky! Now stop — he's as blue as shell fish!

JESSE: Help!

GALY GAY: Out of the circle! She's out of the circle!

POLLY: Well! And what do you all say to that? Have you ever seen such brutality? All I can say is: here unnatural deceit gets its deserts.

Big applause.

POLLY: Elephant Calf, you have grossly deceived yourself. By this brutal pulling, you have proved, not what you intended, but something else, namely, that never never never can you be the son — or daughter — of this unhappy, martyred mother. You have pulled the truth into the light, Jacky my pal!

SOLDIERS: Oho! Great! Hideous! A nice family! Be off, Jacky boy, it's all up with you. A put-up job. Just stand by the truth, Jacky.

POLLY: There, gentlemen: I think that should suffice. The first and last proof, I think you will agree, has been brought to harbor. And now, listen carefully, gentlemen, and let me ask those to listen also who at first thought it necessary to raise a rumpus here, as also those who bet their good pennies that this miserable elephant calf, punctured, as he now is, by proofs, is not a murderer, this elephant calf *is* a murderer! This elephant calf, which is not the daughter of this worthy mother as it contended, but the son, as I have proved, is also not the son, as you have seen, because it is not even the child of this matron, whom it murdered, though she stands here before your very eyes and acts like nothing had happened, which after all is natural, though on the other hand it is unprecedented, which I am also ready to prove, in fact I will prove anything you like, and will contend even more than that, and never be put off but always insist on what I see the way I see it, and prove it too, for, I ask you: what is anything without proof?

The applause ever more tumultuous.

POLLY: Without proof a man is not even a man but an Orang-Utang, as Darwin proved, and then where is progress? And if you so much as bat an eyelash, you miserable, little nothing of a lie-dripping elephant calf — phony to the marrow, as you are — then I will prove anyhow, and I'm going to do it in any case, yes, actually this is my main point, gentlemen, that this elephant calf is not an elephant calf anyhow, but at best Jeraiah Jip of Tipperary.

Tumultuous applause.

SOLDIERS: Hooray!

GALY GAY: That's not right.

POLLY: Why not? Why shouldn't it be right?

GALY GAY: It's not what the play says. Take it back.

POLLY: But you *are* a murderer.

GALY GAY: That's not true.

POLLY: But I've proved it. Proved, proved, proved!

GALY GAY, *moaning, hurls himself at the banana tree. Under this terrific assault, the tree collapses.*

POLLY (*collapsing*): You see! You see!

URIAH: Sò. Now you are a murderer.

POLLY (*with a groan*): And I proved it.

Curtain.

URIAH: The song — quick!

THE FOUR PLAYERS (*get quickly in front of the curtain to sing*):

Oh dear, what fun we had in old Uganda!
A nickel for a chair on the veranda!
Oh dear, the poker games with Mister Tiger!
We did twice as well, I'll tell you that,

When we bet the hide of Daddy Kruger
And Tiger bet his bowler hat!
Oh, dear, the moon shone bright in old Uganda!
The air was cool, the trains went root-toot-toot!
Not every one has got the money
For poker with this very funny
Tiger in his business suit.
(A nickel for a chair on the veranda.)

SOLDIER: It's over? But it's so unjust! Does that make a good ending? You can't just stop there. Leave the curtain up. Go on with the play!

POLLY: What? There's no more script! Be reasonable. The play is over.

SOLDIERS: What gall! I never knew anything like it. Crap of the purest water! Against good sense! (*A bunch of them go up on the stage and talk earnestly.*) We want our money back. Either the elephant calf ends up all right or you'll put our money down on your bar, every red cent of it, you Moon of Cooch Behar!

POLLY: What you saw on this stage was the naked truth, I would have you know.

SOLDIERS: In that case, you are all about to see the whites of truth's eyes!

POLLY: You only say that because you know nothing of Art. You don't know how to behave to artists.

SOLDIERS: We can do without all this talk!

GALY GAY: By the way, I wouldn't like you to think *I* don't accept what you have just seen.

POLLY: Thank you, cap'n.

GALY GAY: And to get ahead of the game a little bit, I would like to invite to a little eight-round boxing match with four-ounce gloves whichever gentleman, whichever bizarre gentleman, asks for his money back with the greatest urgency.

SOLDIERS: That would be Townley. Townley: forward! Wipe this little elephant's little snout off!

GALY GAY: Very well, so we shall now see, I believe, whether it was the truth that we staged here for you, or whether it was theatre — good or bad — my fine fellows!

All off to the boxing match.

THE MEASURES TAKEN

CHARACTERS

Control Chorus

Four Agitators

Young Comrade

Leader

Overseer

Two Coolies

Two Textile Workers

Trader

Policeman

CONTROL CHORUS: Step forward! Your work has been successful. In yet another country the ranks of the fighters are joined, and the revolution marches on. We agree to what you have done.

FOUR AGITATORS: Stop! We have something to say. We announce the death of a comrade.

CONTROL CHORUS: Who killed him?

FOUR AGITATORS: We killed him. We shot him and threw him into a lime pit.

CONTROL CHORUS: Demonstrate how it happened and why, and you will hear our verdict.

FOUR AGITATORS: We shall respect your verdict.

1

THE CLASSICAL WRITINGS

FOUR AGITATORS: We came from Moscow as agitators. We were to travel to the city of Mukden to make propaganda, and build up the Chinese Party in the factories. We were to announce ourselves at the last Party Headquarters from the frontier and demand a guide. In the anteroom a young comrade came to us, and we spoke of the nature of our assignment. We shall repeat what was said.

Three of them stand together. The other, presenting the YOUNG COMRADE, *stands by himself.*

YOUNG COMRADE: I am the secretary at the last Party Headquarters from the frontier. My heart beats for the revolution. The sight of injustice drove me into

77

the ranks of the fighters. I am for freedom. I believe in humanity. And I am for the measures taken
by the Communist Party which fights for the classless
society against exploitation and ignorance.

THREE AGITATORS: We come from Moscow.

YOUNG COMRADE: We expected you.

THREE AGITATORS: Why?

YOUNG COMRADE: We're getting nowhere. There is scarcity
and disorder, little bread and much struggle. Many
are brave, but few can read. Few machines, and no
one understands them. Our locomotives have broken
down. Have you brought any locomotives with you?

THREE AGITATORS: No.

YOUNG COMRADE: Have you any tractors?

THREE AGITATORS: No.

YOUNG COMRADE: Our farmers are still straining their
muscles at old wooden plows. And so we have no
way of putting our fields in order. Have you brought
any seed?

THREE AGITATORS: No.

YOUNG COMRADE: Have you got munitions at least and
machine guns?

THREE AGITATORS: No.

YOUNG COMRADE: There are just two of us to defend the
revolution here. Surely you've brought us a letter
from the Central Committee telling us what to do?

THREE AGITATORS: No.

YOUNG COMRADE: Then you yourselves are going to help
us?

THREE AGITATORS: No.

YOUNG COMRADE: Day and night we never get out of our clothes, in the struggle against hunger, decay, and counterrevolution. Yet you bring us nothing.

THREE AGITATORS: Exactly so: we bring you nothing. But over the frontier to Mukden we bring the Chinese workers the teachings of the classic writers and the propagandists, the ABC of communism; to the ignorant, instruction about their condition; to the oppressed, class consciousness; and to the class conscious, the experience of revolution. From you, however, we are to demand an automobile and a guide.

YOUNG COMRADE: Then I was wrong to ask?

THREE AGITATORS: No, but a good question led to a better answer. We see that everything has already been asked of you. But even more will be asked of you: one of you two must guide us to Mukden.

YOUNG COMRADE: Then I'll leave my post, which was too hard for two, but which one alone must now learn to handle. I shall go with you. Marching forward, spreading the teaching of the communist classics: World Revolution.

CONTROL CHORUS:

Praise of the U.S.S.R.

Certainly our misery
Was something to talk about.
But seated at our sparse table
Was the Hope of all the oppressed
Who is satisfied with water.
And in a clear voice
Behind the broken-down door
Knowledge taught the guests.
When the doors are broken
We only become visible from a little further away

We whom frost does not kill, nor hunger
Untiringly conferring about
The world's destinies.

FOUR AGITATORS: In this way, the Young Comrade of the
frontier station agreed to the general character of
our work and we came — four men and one woman
— before the leader at Party Headquarters.

2

THE BLOTTING OUT

FOUR AGITATORS: But the work in Mukden was illegal, so, before we crossed the frontier, we had to blot out our faces. Our Young Comrade agreed to this. We will repeat the incident.

One of the AGITATORS *presents the* LEADER *at Party Headquarters.*

LEADER: I am the Leader at the last headquarters. I have agreed that the comrade from my station should go along as guide. But there is unrest in the Mukden factories. At the present time the eyes of the world are on this city to see if one of us won't be found leaving a Chinese worker's hut. And I hear that gunboats stand ready on the rivers and armored trains in the sidings, ready to attack us at once, if one of us is seen there. And so I am having the comrades cross the frontier as Chinese. (*To the* AGITATORS:) You must not be seen.

TWO AGITATORS: We shall not be seen.

LEADER: If one of you is wounded, he must not be found.

TWO AGITATORS: He will not be found.

LEADER: Then you are ready to die and to hide the dead one?

TWO AGITATORS: Yes.

LEADER: Then you are yourselves no longer. You are not Karl Schmitt from Berlin, you are not Anna Kjersk from Kazan, and you are not Peter Sawitch from Moscow. One and all of you are nameless and motherless, blank pages on which the revolution writes its instructions.

TWO AGITATORS: Yes.

LEADER (*gives them masks; they put them on*): Then, from this time on, you are no one no longer. From this time on, and probably until you disappear, you are unknown workers, fighters, Chinese, born of Chinese mothers, with yellow skin, speaking Chinese in fever and in sleep.

TWO AGITATORS: Yes.

LEADER: In the interests of communism, agreeing to the advance of the proletarian masses of all lands, saying Yes to the revolutionizing of the world.

TWO AGITATORS: Yes. And in the way the Young Comrade demonstrated his agreement to the blotting-out of his face.

CONTROL CHORUS: Who fights for communism must be able to fight and not to fight; to speak the truth and not to speak the truth; to perform services and not to perform services; to keep promises and not to keep promises; to go into danger and to keep out of danger; to be recognizable and not to be recognizable. Who fights for communism has only one of all the virtues: that he fights for communism.

FOUR AGITATORS: As Chinese, we went to Mukden, four men and one woman, to make propaganda and support the Chinese workers through the teachings of the classics and the propagandists, the ABC of communism: to bring to the ignorant instruction about their situation; to the oppressed, class-consciousness; and to the class-conscious, the experience of revolution.

CONTROL CHORUS:

Praise of Illegal Work

It is splendid
To take up the word as a weapon in the class war
To rouse the masses to the fight in a loud and ringing
    voice
To crush the oppressors
To free the oppressed.
Hard and useful is the small daily labor
The grim, persistent tying and spreading of the Party's
    net
For the capitalists' guns
To speak
But conceal the speaker
To win the victory
But conceal the victor
To die
But hide the death.
Who would not do much for fame
But who would do it for silence?
Yet the impoverished host invites Honor to supper
And out of the tiny and tumble-down hut steps
    irresistibly
Greatness
And Fame calls in vain
On the doers of the great deed.

FOUR AGITATORS: In the city of Mukden, we made propaganda among the workers. We had no bread for the
hungry but only knowledge for the ignorant. Therefore we spoke of the root cause of poverty, did not
abolish poverty, but spoke of the abolition of the
root cause.

3

THE STONE

FOUR AGITATORS: First, we went down into the lower
section of the city. Coolies were dragging a barge
with a rope. But the ground on the bank was slippery.
So when one of them slipped, and the overseer hit
him, we said to the Young Comrade: "Go after them,
make propaganda among them after work. But don't
give way to pity!" And we asked: "Do you agree to
it?" And he agreed to it and hurried away and at
once gave way to pity. We will show you.

TWO AGITATORS *present* COOLIES, *fastening a rope to
a hook, and then pulling the rope over their shoulders.
One presents the* YOUNG COMRADE, *one the* OVER-
SEER.

TWO COOLIES: We are the coolies and we pull the rice
barge up the river.

CONTROL CHORUS:

Song of the Rice Barge Coolies

In the city up the river
A mouthful of rice awaits us
But the barge is heavy that we must pull up the river
And the water flows down the river
We shall never get there
    Pull faster
    We want our dinner
    Pull evenly
    Don't jostle the next man

In the barge is rice
The farmer who grew it received a few cents

We get even less
An ox would cost more
Than we do
There are too many of us
> Pull faster
> We want our dinner
> Pull evenly
> Don't jostle the next man

Night will soon fall
A resting place smaller than a dog's shadow
Costs us a mouthful of rice
Because the river bank is slippery
We are making no headway
> Pull faster
> We want our dinner
> Pull evenly
> Don't jostle the next man

YOUNG COMRADE: It is repulsive to hear how the torture of these men's labor is masked by beauty!

OVERSEER: I am the Overseer. I must get the rice to the city by evening. Pull faster.

CONTROL CHORUS:
Our fathers pulled the barge from the river mouth
A little farther upstream
Our children will reach the source
We come between
> Pull faster
> We want our dinner
> Pull evenly
> Don't jostle the next man

ONE COOLIE (*slipping out of line*): I can't keep going.

CONTROL CHORUS (*while the* COOLIES *stand and are whipped*):

The rope that cuts into our shoulders
Holds longer than we do
The Overseer's whip has seen four generations
We are not the last
    Pull faster
    We want our dinner
    Pull evenly
    Don't jostle the next man

YOUNG COMRADE: It is hard to see these men without pity. (*To the* OVERSEER:) Can't you see the ground is slippery?

OVERSEER: The ground is what?

YOUNG COMRADE: Slippery! (*To the* COOLIE:) I now take a stone and lay it in the mud. Now walk!

CONTROL CHORUS:
When the rice arrives in the city
And children ask who dragged the heavy barge
The answer given is:
The barge was dragged
    Pull faster
    We want our dinner
    Pull evenly
    Don't jostle the next man

OVERSEER: What? You claim this bank is so slippery it's impossible to pull a barge full of rice?

YOUNG COMRADE: I've only put a stone there for this man.

OVERSEER: Then you think we can't pull the barge without you? Or that the city of Mukden doesn't need rice?

YOUNG COMRADE: The men can't pull the barge if they fall down.

OVERSEER: Should I provide a stone for each of them to walk on — from here to the city of Mukden?

YOUNG COMRADE: I don't know what *you* should do, but
I know what *they* should do.
The food from down there
Feeds people up here
Those who brought it up for them
Have not fed

COOLIE (*to* OVERSEER): This fellow's a fool. They all
laugh at him.

OVERSEER: No, he's one of those that stir up the workers.
Hello there! Hold that man!

FOUR AGITATORS: And they at once took hold of him.
And they pursued him for two days till he met us.
Then they pursued us and him together in the city
of Mukden for a whole week. They wouldn't let us
get near the central section of the city.

DISCUSSION

CONTROL CHORUS:
But is it not right to support the weak man
And help him wherever he confronts us?
To help the exploited man
In his daily hardships and oppressed as he is?

FOUR AGITATORS: He did not help him. But he did hinder
us from making propaganda in our section of the city.

CONTROL CHORUS: We agree to that.

FOUR AGITATORS: The Young Comrade perceived that he
had put his feelings above his understanding. But we
comforted him and spoke to him the words of Comrade Lenin:

CONTROL CHORUS:
Intelligence is not to make no mistakes
But quickly to see how to make them good.

4

JUSTICE

FOUR AGITATORS: We founded the first Party cells in the factories and trained the first functionaries, established a Party school and taught them how to make the forbidden literature secretly available. Then we spread propaganda in the textile works, and each man had his assignment, and we said to the Young Comrade: "Place yourself at the factory door and hand out leaflets, but don't give yourself away." Then suspicion fell upon a man who stood near him and was seized in his stead. And he could not keep quiet. We will show it.

THREE AGITATORS: With the barge workers you failed.

YOUNG COMRADE: Yes.

THREE AGITATORS: Did that teach you something?

YOUNG COMRADE: Yes.

THREE AGITATORS: Will you handle yourself better with the textile workers?

YOUNG COMRADE: Yes.

Two agitators play TEXTILE WORKERS.

TWO TEXTILE WORKERS: We are workers in the textile works.

CONTROL CHORUS:

The Song of the Textile Workers

Today once again
There was less money in the pay envelope

> If we leave the looms
> Others will take our places
> We cannot leave.

YOUNG COMRADE: Strike! Your wages are too low. Leave your looms! Place yourselves at the gates and let no one get to your looms!

CONTROL CHORUS:
> If we place ourselves in the gateways and
> Let no one get to our looms
> The soldiers will come and shoot at us
> We cannot place ourselves in the gateways.

YOUNG COMRADE: Strike! Your wages are too low. Place yourselves in the gateways and fight the soldiers!

CONTROL CHORUS:
> Who will be first to go hungry? Who first
> Will set his face against the guns? Who
> Will begin? Who will be able
> To eat his supper?

YOUNG COMRADE: Strike! Your wages are too low. All begin together. Every man must be the first man!

TWO TEXTILE WORKERS: When the factory closes, we're going home. We are very dissatisfied but we don't know what to do.

YOUNG COMRADE (*sticking a leaflet in front of one of them, the other stands inactive*): Read it and pass it on. When you've read it, you'll know what to do.

FIRST TEXTILE WORKER *takes it and walks on.*

One of the agitators plays a POLICEMAN.

POLICEMAN: I am a policeman and get my bread from the ruling class for combating discontent. (*He takes the leaflet away from the* FIRST TEXTILE WORKER.) Who gave you that leaflet?

FIRST TEXTILE WORKER: I don't know. Somebody just stuck it in my hand as I was passing.

POLICEMAN (*stepping up to the* SECOND TEXTILE WORKER). *You* gave him the leaflet! We have orders to hunt up the ones that give out the leaflets.

SECOND TEXTILE WORKER: I didn't give out any leaflet.

YOUNG COMRADE: Is it a crime to teach them they are ignorant of their situation?

POLICEMAN: These teachings lead to God knows what. Teach a factory that sort of stuff, and they don't know who the owner is any more. This little leaflet is more dangerous than ten cannon.

YOUNG COMRADE: What's in it?

POLICEMAN: How would I know? (*To the* SECOND TEXTILE WORKER:) What's in it?

SECOND TEXTILE WORKER: I don't know the leaflet. I didn't hand it out.

YOUNG COMRADE: I know he didn't.

POLICEMAN (*to* YOUNG COMRADE): Did *you* give him the leaflet?

YOUNG COMRADE: No.

POLICEMAN (*to* SECOND TEXTILE WORKER): Then *you* gave it to him.

YOUNG COMRADE (*to* FIRST TEXTILE WORKER): What'll happen to him?

FIRST TEXTILE WORKER: He could be shot.

YOUNG COMRADE: What do you want to shoot him for? Aren't you a proletarian, too, policeman?

POLICEMAN (*to* SECOND TEXTILE WORKER): Come with me. (*Strikes him on the head.*)

YOUNG COMRADE (*trying to stop him*): It wasn't him.

POLICEMAN: Then it *was* you!

SECOND TEXTILE WORKER: It wasn't him.

POLICEMAN: Then it was the both of you!

FIRST TEXTILE WORKER: Run, you fool, run, your pocket's full of leaflets!

POLICEMAN *cuts the* SECOND TEXTILE WORKER *down.*

YOUNG COMRADE (*pointing at* POLICEMAN. *To the* FIRST TEXTILE WORKER): He's killed an innocent man. You are a witness.

FIRST TEXTILE WORKER (*attacking the* POLICEMAN): Hireling!

POLICEMAN *draws his revolver.*

YOUNG COMRADE *grabs the* POLICEMAN *by the neck from behind. The* FIRST TEXTILE WORKER *twists his arm back slowly. The shot goes wild. The* POLICEMAN *is disarmed.*

YOUNG COMRADE (*yelling*): Help, Comrades! Help! They're shooting innocent bystanders!

FOUR AGITATORS: The workers at once came running out of the factories to demonstrate against police violence. That is how the textile workers' strike arose. But the coolie organization demanded the punishment of the policeman, and the policeman was punished. But the strike was discontinued for a long time, and the guards were reinforced in the factories. Everyone talked about the murder of the innocent man; but we were banished from the factories.

DISCUSSION

CONTROL CHORUS: But is it not right to act justly and always to combat injustice wherever it may be found?

FOUR AGITATORS: In order to uphold the great injustice the small justice was conceded. But the great strike was knocked out of our hands.

CONTROL CHORUS: We agree to that.

5

WHAT IS A HUMAN BEING ACTUALLY?

FOUR AGITATORS: Daily we fought those old associates: oppression and despair. We taught the workers to transform a struggle for higher wages into a struggle for power. Taught them the use of weapons and the art of street fighting. Then we heard there was conflict between the merchants and the British, who ruled the city, on account of tariffs. In order to exploit this rulers' quarrel for the benefit of the ruled, we sent the Young Comrade with a letter to the richest of merchants. It said: "Arm the coolies!" We said to the Young Comrade: "Win his confidence." But when the food came on the table, he didn't keep his mouth shut. We will show you.

THREE AGITATORS: In the spinning mills you failed.

YOUNG COMRADE: Yes.

THREE AGITATORS: Did you learn something by it?

YOUNG COMRADE: Yes.

THREE AGITATORS: Will you bring arms from the merchants?

YOUNG COMRADE: Yes.

An agitator as TRADER.

TRADER: I am the trader. I'm expecting a letter from the coolie organization about the possibility of our getting together against the British.

YOUNG COMRADE: Here is the letter from the coolie organization.

TRADER: Please come and dine with me.

YOUNG COMRADE: It's an honor for me to be permitted to dine with you.

TRADER: While dinner's being prepared, I'd like to give you my opinion of coolies. Please sit down over here.

YOUNG COMRADE: I'm very interested in your opinion.

TRADER: Why do I get everything cheaper than anyone else? And why would a coolie work for me almost without pay?

YOUNG COMRADE: I don't know.

TRADER: Because I'm bright. You're pretty bright yourselves or how would you squeeze union dues out of your coolies?

YOUNG COMRADE: That's true. — Incidentally, are you going to arm the coolies against the British?

TRADER: Maybe, maybe. — I know how to handle a coolie. You must give him enough rice to keep him from dying. Otherwise, you can't get any work out of him. Is that right?

YOUNG COMRADE: Yes. That is right.

TRADER: I say it is not right. If coolies are cheaper than rice, I can get me a new coolie. Isn't that nearer the truth?

YOUNG COMRADE: Yes, that's nearer the truth. — Incidentally, when will you start sending weapons into our section of the city?

TRADER: Soon, soon. — You couldn't help noticing that the coolies who load my leather eat my rice in the canteen?

YOUNG COMRADE: I couldn't help noticing.

TRADER: What do you think: do I pay a lot for the work?

YOUNG COMRADE: No, but your rice is expensive, and you insist on the work being well done, and your rice is bad rice.

TRADER: You people are bright.

YOUNG COMRADE: And when will you arm the coolies against the British?

TRADER: After dinner we can inspect the arsenal. Now I'm going to sing you my favorite song.

The Song of Supply and Demand

Down the river there is rice
In the provinces up the river people need rice:
If we leave the rice in the warehouses
The rice will cost them more
Those who pull the rice barge will then get less rice
And rice will be even cheaper for me
    What is rice actually?
    Do I know what rice is?
    God knows what rice is!
    I don't know what rice is!
    I only know its price

Winter comes, the people need clothing
One must buy up the cotton
And not let go of it
When the cold weather comes, clothing will cost more
The cotton-spinning mills pay too high wages
There's too much cotton around anyway
    What is cotton actually?
    Do I know what cotton is?
    God knows what cotton is!
    I don't know what cotton is
    I only know its price

Likewise men — they need too much food
And so men get to cost more

To make the food, men are needed
Cooks make the food cheaper
But those who eat it make it cost more
There aren't enough men around anyway.
    What is a man actually?
    Do I know what a man is?
    God knows what a man is!
    I don't know what a man is
    I only know his price
(*To the* YOUNG COMRADE:)
And now we're going to eat my good rice.

YOUNG COMRADE (*stands up*): I can't eat with you.

FOUR AGITATORS: That's what he said. And neither threats
nor laughter could bring him to eat with a man he
despised. And the trader drove him out of the house,
and the coolies were not armed.

DISCUSSION

CONTROL CHORUS: But isn't it right to put honor before
everything else?

FOUR AGITATORS: No.

CONTROL CHORUS: We agree to that

Change the World, It Needs It

With whom would the right-minded man not sit
To help the right?
What medicine would taste too bad
To a dying man?
What baseness would you not commit
To root out baseness?
If, finally, you could change the world
What task would you be too good for?
Sink down in the filth
Embrace the butcher

But change the world: it needs it!
Who are you?
Stinking, be gone from
The room that has been cleaned! Would that
You were the last of the filth which
You had to remove!

FOUR AGITATORS: Yet in those days we managed to spread
the net of the Party for the capitalists' guns.

6

REBELLION AGAINST THE TEACHING

FOUR AGITATORS: That week the persecutions sharply increased. All we had left was a secret room for the hectograph machine and the pamphlets. On the evening of the third day, reaching our retreat not without risk, we found the Young Comrade in the doorway. And there were bundles in front of the house in the rain. We shall repeat what was said.

THREE AGITATORS: What are these bundles?

YOUNG COMRADE: Our propaganda.

THREE AGITATORS: What are you going to do with it?

YOUNG COMRADE: I have something to tell you. The new leaders of the unemployed came here today and convinced me that we begin by taking action — right away. We want to hand out the propaganda leaflets. We led off by calling for a general strike.

THREE AGITATORS: Now you have betrayed us four times over.

YOUNG COMRADE: Poverty is spreading, unrest is growing in the city.

THREE AGITATORS: The ignorant are beginning to recognize their situation.

YOUNG COMRADE: The unemployed have adopted our teaching.

THREE AGITATORS: The oppressed are learning class consciousness.

YOUNG COMRADE: They go out into the streets and want to demolish the spinning mills.

THREE AGITATORS: The roads to revolution show themselves. Our responsibility increases. And at this point you place the propaganda leaflets at the door so everyone can see them!

YOUNG COMRADE: The unemployed can wait no longer
Nor can I
Wait any longer
There are too many paupers.

THREE AGITATORS: But not enough fighters.

YOUNG COMRADE: Their sufferings are enormous.

THREE AGITATORS: It is not enough to suffer.

YOUNG COMRADE: Inside with us here are seven who came to us representing the unemployed. Behind them stand seven thousand and they know: Unhappiness doesn't grow on the chest like leprosy. Poverty won't fall off the roof like a loose tile, no: poverty and unhappiness are man's doing. Scarcity is all the meat in their oven, and their own wailing is all they have to eat! But they know all this.

THREE AGITATORS: Do they know how many regiments the government has?

YOUNG COMRADE: No.

THREE AGITATORS: Then they know too little. Where are your weapons?

YOUNG COMRADE (*showing his hands*): We shall fight tooth and nail!

THREE AGITATORS: Tooth and nail won't suffice. Therefore hear this: on orders from the Party, we have spoken about the situation with the coolie organization which leads the working masses, and we have decided to postpone armed action till the delegates of the farmers' organizations have arrived in the city.

YOUNG COMRADE: Then hear what *I* say: I see with my two eyes that poverty cannot wait. I see how easily, if we do nothing, they run away and go home. I therefore set my face against your decision to wait.

THREE AGITATORS:
Do not see with your own eyes!
The individual has two eyes
The Party has a thousand eyes
The Party sees seven states
The individual sees one city
The individual has his hour
But the Party has many hours.
The individual can be wiped out
But the Party cannot be wiped out
For it rests on the teaching of the classic writers
Which is created from acquaintance with reality
And is destined to change it
For the teaching will take hold of the masses.

YOUNG COMRADE: Let me ask this: is it in line with the classic writers to let misery wait?

THREE AGITATORS: They speak, not of pity, but of the deed which does away with pity.

YOUNG COMRADE: Then the classic writers don't advocate helping every poor man at once and putting that before everything else?

THREE AGITATORS: No.

YOUNG COMRADE: Then the classic writers are dirt. I tear them up. For man, living man, cries out. His misery tears down the dikes of mere teaching. And that's why I'm going into action — right now, this minute! For *I* cry out too. *I* tear down the dikes of the teaching! (*He tears up the writings.*)

THREE AGITATORS:
Do not tear them!
We need every one of them.

Take a look at reality!
Your revolution is quickly made and lasts one day
And is strangled the morning after
But our revolution begins tomorrow
Conquers and changes the world.
Your revolution stops when you stop.
When you have stopped
Our revolution marches on.

CONTROL CHORUS:

Praise of the Party

The individual has two eyes
The Party has a thousand eyes
The Party sees seven states
The individual sees one city
The individual has his hour
But the Party has many hours
A single man can be wiped out
But the Party cannot be wiped out
For it rests on the teaching of the classic writers
Which is created from acquaintance with reality
And is destined to change it
For the teaching will take hold of the masses.

YOUNG COMRADE: That's no good any more. Looking at the struggle as it is now, I throw away all that was good yesterday, I reject every agreement *with* everybody and do what alone is human. Here is action. I place myself at the head of it. My heart beats for the revolution, and the revolution is here!

THREE AGITATORS: Silence!

YOUNG COMRADE: The sight of injustice drove me into the ranks of the fighters. Here is injustice.

THREE AGITATORS: Silence!

YOUNG COMRADE: Here is oppression. I am for freedom!

THREE AGITATORS: Silence! You are betraying us.

YOUNG COMRADE:
>   I have seen too much.
>   I shall therefore go before them
>   As what I am
>   And state
>   What is.

He takes off his mask and shouts.

>   We have come to help you!
>   We come from Moscow!

He tears up the mask.

FOUR AGITATORS:
>   And we saw him and in the twilight saw
>   His naked face, human, open, guileless.
>   He had torn up his mask.
>   And the exploited shouted from their houses:
>   "Who disturbs the sleep of the poor?"
>   And a window opened and a voice shouted:
>   "Foreigners! Throw the troublemakers out!"
>   We were now recognizable.
>   And in that hour we heard of unrest in the lower
>   section of the city
>   And the ignorant waited in the meeting houses and
>   The unarmed in the streets.
>   And we struck him down
>   And lifted him up and left the city in haste.

7

FINAL PURSUIT AND ANALYSIS

CONTROL CHORUS: They left the city!
Unrest grows in the city
But the leadership flees over the city line.
What measures did you take?

FOUR AGITATORS: Wait a moment. When in the course of our flight we came near the lime pits outside the city limits, we saw our pursuers behind us.

CONTROL CHORUS:
They run like race horses.
The factory councils come to the central office for consultation
But the shelterless slept on the propaganda leaflets.
What measures did you take?

FOUR AGITATORS: Wait a moment. Yes, even now we helped him. Helped him along till we reached the lime pits.

CONTROL CHORUS:
The masses wait in the meeting houses
But the speakers are off at the mines.
What measures did you take?

FOUR AGITATORS: Wait a moment.
It is easy to know what is right
Far from the shooting
When you have months of time
But we
Had ten minutes' time and
Enemy guns to think of and
Had to see the face of the unhappy one
Our comrade.

CONTROL CHORUS: Your measure! Your measure!

FOUR AGITATORS: Wait a moment.
    As even an animal
    Will help an animal
    We too wished to help
    Him who fought for our cause at our side.

CONTROL CHORUS:
    In time of extreme persecution and
    The confusion of theory
    The fighters depict the structure of the situation
    And weigh the stakes and the possibilities.

FOUR AGITATORS: We did just that.

THE ANALYSIS

FIRST AGITATOR: The masses are in the streets, we said.

SECOND AGITATOR: But we must assemble them in meetings.

THIRD AGITATOR: Or they won't know what to do, and will disperse, before the delegates of the farmers' organizations have arrived in the city.

SECOND AGITATOR: Therefore we cannot get our comrade over the border.

THIRD AGITATOR: But if we hide him and he later reappears, what happens when he is recognized?

FIRST AGITATOR: There were gunboats on the rivers and armored trains in the railroad sidings, ready to attack whenever one of us was found. He must not be found.

FOUR AGITATORS:
    If we are found, no matter where,
    The cry goes up: "The rulers are in danger
    Of annihilation!"
    And the cannon fire.

Wherever the starving groan and hit back
Their tormentors shout
That we have bribed them
To groan and hit back.

CONTROL CHORUS:
It is written on our foreheads
That we are against exploitation.
In the letter of information against us is written:
"They are for the oppressed!"

Who helps the despairing
Passes for the scum of the earth
We are the scum of the earth
We must not be found.

8

THE INTERMENT

THREE AGITATORS:
>We decided:
>Then he must disappear, and totally.
>For we must return to our work
>And cannot take him with us and cannot leave him behind
>We must therefore shoot him and throw him in the lime pit
>For the lime will burn him.
>We will repeat our last conversation
>And demand your verdict.

FIRST AGITATOR: We are going to ask him if he agrees, for he was a brave fighter.

SECOND AGITATOR: But even if he does not agree, he must disappear, and totally.

FIRST AGITATOR (*to the* YOUNG COMRADE): We must shoot you and throw you in the lime pit so the lime will burn you. And we ask you: do you agree to this?

YOUNG COMRADE: Yes.

THREE AGITATORS: He said Yes.

CONTROL CHORUS: His answer was in accord with reality. Did you find no way out, whereby the young fighter might be preserved to fight again?

FOUR AGITATORS:
>The time was short. We
>Found no way out.
>In sight of our pursuers
>We reflected for five minutes
>On a better possibility.

You too, think now about
A better possibility.

Pause.

Lamenting, we beat our heads with our fists
Since they had only this fearful counsel to offer:
   forthwith
To cut off a foot from our own body for
IT IS A FEARSOME THING TO KILL.
But we will kill ourselves and not just others if
   necessary
Since only by force can this dying world be changed
As every living man knows.
It is not granted to us, we said,
Not to kill.
At one with the inflexible will to change the world
We formulated
The measures to be taken.

CONTROL CHORUS:
   Go on with the story
   You are assured of our sympathy
   It was not easy to do what was right.

THREE AGITATORS: Where shall we put you, we asked him.

YOUNG COMRADE: In the lime pit, he said.

THREE AGITATORS: We asked: Will you do it alone?

YOUNG COMRADE: Help me.

THREE AGITATORS:
   We said: lean your head on our arms
   Close your eyes
   We will carry you.

YOUNG COMRADE (*unseen*):
   He then said:
   "In the interests of communism
   Agreeing to the advance of the proletarian masses of
      all lands
   Saying Yes to the revolutionizing of the world."

THREE AGITATORS:
Then we shot him
And threw him down into the lime pit
And when the lime had devoured him
We returned to our work.

CONTROL CHORUS:
And your work was successful
You have spread
The teachings of the classics
The ABC of communism:
To the ignorant, instruction about their situation
To the oppressed, class consciousness
And to the class conscious, the experience of
    revolution.
In yet another country the revolution advances
In another land the ranks of the fighters are joined
We agree to what you have done.

THE EXCEPTION
AND THE RULE

CHARACTERS

Merchant

Guide

Coolie

Two Policemen

Innkeeper

Widow

Leader of the Second Caravan

Judge

Two Colleagues

THE ACTORS:
> We hereby report to you
> The story of a journey, undertaken by
> One who exploits and two who are exploited
> Observe the conduct of these people closely:
> Find it estranging even if not very strange
> Hard to explain even if it is the custom
> Hard to understand even if it is the rule
> Observe the smallest action, seeming simple,
> With mistrust
> Inquire if a thing be necessary
> Especially if it is common
> We particularly ask you —
> When a thing continually occurs —
> Not on that account to find it natural
> Let nothing be called natural
> In an age of bloody confusion
> Ordered disorder, planned caprice,
> And dehumanized humanity, lest all things
> Be held unalterable!

SCENE 1

THE RACE THROUGH THE DESERT

*Two separate little parties, at some distance from each
other, are crossing the desert at speed.*

MERCHANT (*to his men, a* GUIDE *and a* COOLIE, *the latter
laden with baggage*): Hurry, you lazy dogs! In another two days we've got to be at Station Han. We've
got to squeeze out a head start of one full day! (*To
the audience*:) I am the merchant Karl Langmann.
I'm on my way to Urga to make the final arrange-
ments for a concession. My competitors aren't very
far behind, and whoever gets there first closes the
deal. By my cleverness, my energetic surmounting of
every obstacle, and my uncompromising attitude to
the personnel, I have made the first part of the
journey in half the usual time. Unfortunately, so
have my competitors. (*He looks toward the rear
through binoculars. To his men*:) Look, they're on
our heels again already! (*To the* GUIDE *only*:) Why
don't you drive the fellow on? I hired you to drive
him hard, not to take a walk with him on my money.
All right: if there's any sabotage, I'll report you —
at the employment agency in Urga.

GUIDE (*to the* COOLIE): Make an effort. Faster!

MERCHANT: You don't have the right tone of voice, you'll
never be a real guide. I should have taken a more
expensive one, they always repay your investment.
Go on then: hit the fellow! (*To the audience*:) I'm
not for beating but right now there's no other way:
if I don't get there first, I'm ruined. (*To the* GUIDE:)
Confess: this carrier's your brother — *some* relation
anyhow — *that's* why you don't beat him! I know
you, though, I know you all from way back, and you

112

aren't such gentle Jesuses either! Beat him or you're fired — and you can sue me for your wages! For God's sake, they'll overtake us!

COOLIE (*to the* GUIDE): Beat me, keep some of your strength in reserve. I must keep some of *my* strength in reserve if we are supposed to reach Station Han.

The GUIDE *beats the* COOLIE.

SHOUTS FROM THE REAR: Hello! Is this the way to Urga! We're friends! Wait for us!

MERCHANT (*neither answering nor looking back*): To hell with you! Let's go! I'll have kept my men going three days, two with curses, the third with promises, and we'll see about the promises in Urga. My competitors are at my heels, but the second night I'll keep going all night, I'll get so far ahead they can't see me, and we'll be at Station Han on the third day, one day ahead of all the others! (*He sings.*)

As I did not sleep
I soon took the lead.
As I kept on the move
I am now far ahead.
The weak lag behind
But the strong arrive.

SCENE 2

THE END OF A MUCH-TRAVELED ROAD

MERCHANT (*before Station Han*): Here is Station Han. Thank God I've reached it one day ahead of all the others. My men are exhausted. What's more, they're pretty bitter about me. They're just not interested in record-breaking. They're not fighters. They're stick-in-the-muds, nobodies, riffraff! Of course they don't dare say anything because there's still the police, thank God, to maintain order.

TWO POLICEMEN (*approaching*): Everything in order, sir? Satisfied with the roads? Satisfied with the personnel?

MERCHANT: Everything's in order. I made it up to here in three days instead of four. The roads are filthy but I'm a man that finishes what he sets out to do. How are the roads after Station Han? What's in store for us?

TWO POLICEMEN: The uninhabited Jahi desert, sir.

MERCHANT: Is there a police escort to be had there?

TWO POLICEMEN (*passing on*): No, sir, we're the last patrol you'll see, sir.

SCENE 3

THE DISMISSAL OF THE GUIDE
AT STATION HAN

GUIDE: Since we spoke to the police in the street in front
of the station, our merchant is a changed man. The
tone he takes with us is quite different: he's friendly.
This has nothing to do with the speed of the journey
because we're not getting a day off even at this station,
which is the last before the Jahi desert. I don't know
how I'm to get this carrier all the way to Urga in
such an exhausted state. All in all, this friendly behavior on the Merchant's part is very disturbing.
It suggests to me he's working something up.
He walks around lost in thought. Meditations —
machinations! And whatever he cooks up, the carrier
and I will just have to take it. Otherwise he'll either
not pay us or simply throw us over in mid-desert.

MERCHANT (*approaching*): Have some tobacco. Here's
cigarette paper. You'd go through fire for a single
drag, wouldn't you? I don't know what you people
wouldn't do to get this smoke in your throats.
Thank God we've brought enough along. Our tobacco
would take us three times as far as Urga.

GUIDE (*taking the tobacco, aside*): *Our* tobacco!

MERCHANT: Let's sit down, my friend. Why don't you sit
down? Travel brings people into a more intimate
relationship. Of course if you don't wish to, you
may stand. You people have your ways! In general
I wouldn't sit down with you and you wouldn't sit
down with the carrier. The world is based on such
distinctions. But we can smoke together. Can't we?
(*He laughs.*) I like that about you. In its way it's
a kind of dignity. Very well, pack up the rest of the
stuff. And don't forget the water. I hear there aren't

115

many water holes in the desert. Another thing, my friend, I wanted to warn you: did you notice the look the carrier gave you when you handled him roughly? There was something in his eyes that bodes no good. But you'll have to handle him different in the next few days, we have to increase our speed still more. He's a lazy fellow, that one. The region we're coming to is uninhabited; maybe he'll show his true colors. Now you are a better man, you earn more and you don't have to do any carrying: reason enough for him to hate you. You'd be well-advised to keep away from him.

The GUIDE *goes through an open door into the courtyard. The* MERCHANT *is left sitting alone.*

Funny people!

The MERCHANT *is silent and stays where he is. In the yard the* GUIDE *supervises the carrier's packing. Then he sits down and smokes. When the* COOLIE *is ready, he too sits down, receives from his companion tobacco and cigarette paper, and starts a conversation with him.*

COOLIE: The Merchant always says it's a "service to humanity" to take oil out of the ground. When the oil is taken out of the ground, there'll be railroads here, and prosperity will spread. The Merchant says there'll be railroads. How shall I earn my living?

GUIDE: Don't worry. There won't be railroads as fast as all that. They discover oil, and then they suppress the discovery, or so I've heard. The man who stops up the oil-hole gets hush money. That's why the Merchant is in such a hurry. It's not the oil he's after, it's the hush money.

COOLIE: I don't understand.

GUIDE: No one understands.

COOLIE: The path across the desert is sure to get even worse. I hope my feet will hold out.

GUIDE: Certainly.

COOLIE: Are there bandits?

GUIDE: We'll have to keep a lookout — especially today, the first day of the trip. The station attracts every sort of rabble.

COOLIE: How about afterward?

GUIDE: Once we have the Myr river behind us, it's a matter of sticking to the water holes.

COOLIE: You know the way?

GUIDE: Yes.

The MERCHANT *has heard voices. He comes up behind the door to listen.*

COOLIE: Is the Myr river hard to cross?

GUIDE: Not in general — at this time of year. But when it's in flood, the current is very strong, and you take your life in your hands.

MERCHANT: So he's talking to the carrier. He can sit down with *him*. He's smoking with him!

COOLIE: What do you do then?

GUIDE: You often have to wait a week or so to get safely across.

MERCHANT: Well, well, well! He even advises him to take his time and hold on to his precious life! A dangerous fellow, that one. He'd only back his Coolie up. In any case, not the man to put the job through. No telling what he might do either. In short: as of today, they're two against one. At any rate, it's clear he's afraid to boss his own underlings now we're entering uninhabited territory. I must definitely get rid of the fellow. (*He joins the other two.*) I gave you the assignment of checking if the things are properly packed. Let's see how you carry out my assignments. (*He takes hold of a strap and gives it a terrific pull. It breaks.*) Call that packing? Breaking a strap means a day's delay. But that's just what you want: delay!

GUIDE: I do not want delay. And the straps don't break if you don't pull at them like that.

MERCHANT: What? Is the strap broken or not? Just you dare tell me to my face it's not broken! You are unreliable. I made a mistake treating you decently, you people don't appreciate it. I've no use for a guide who can't command the respect of the personnel. It seems to me you should be a carrier, not a guide. There are grounds for believing you stir up the personnel.

GUIDE: What grounds?

MERCHANT: You'd like to know, wouldn't you? Very well: you're dismissed!

GUIDE: But you can't dismiss me when we're halfway there.

MERCHANT: Think yourself lucky if I don't report you at the agency in Urga. Here are your wages, up to this point of course. (*Shouts to the* INNKEEPER *who enters.*) You are my witness: I paid him his wages. (*To the* GUIDE:) And let me tell you something: you'd better not show your face in Urga any more! (*Looks him over from top to toe.*) You'll never get anywhere. (*He goes into the other room with the* INNKEEPER.) I set out at once. If anything happens to me, you are my witness that today I set out alone with that man (*pointing to the* COOLIE). (*The* INNKEEPER *indicates with gestures that he understands nothing. The* MERCHANT *is taken aback. To the audience:*) He doesn't understand. In that case there'll be no one to say where I went. And the worst of it is these fellows *know* there'll be no one. *He sits down and writes a letter*.)

GUIDE (*to the* COOLIE): I made a mistake sitting down with you. Take care: he's bad, that man. (*He gives him his water flask*.) Keep this flask in reserve. Hide it. If you get lost — and you will — he's sure to take yours. I'll explain the road to you.

COOLIE: I don't think you should. He mustn't hear you talking to me. If he throws me out, I'm done for. He doesn't even have to pay me. I'm not in a union like you, I must put up with everything.

MERCHANT (*to the* INNKEEPER): Give this letter to the people who'll be arriving here tomorrow on their way to Urga. I'm going on ahead with my carrier and no one else.

INNKEEPER (*nodding and taking the letter*): But he isn't a guide.

MERCHANT (*to himself*): So he does understand, he just didn't want to admit it. He knows how things are, he simply has no intention of being a witness in such cases. (*To the* INNKEEPER, *peremptorily*:) Explain the way to Urga to my carrier.

The INNKEEPER *goes outside and explains the way to Urga to the* COOLIE. *The* COOLIE *nods eagerly a number of times.*

I see there'll be a struggle. (*He takes out his revolver and cleans it, singing.*)

Sick men die
But strong men fight.
Why should the earth give up its oil,
And why should this coolie carry my baggage?
To get the oil we have to struggle
Both with the earth and with the coolie.

And the meaning of the struggle is this:
Sick men die
But strong men fight.

(*He goes into the courtyard, ready to leave.*) Do you
know the way now?

COOLIE: Yes, Master.

MERCHANT: Then let's go.

The MERCHANT *and the* COOLIE *go. The* INNKEEPER
and the GUIDE *watch.*

GUIDE: I don't know if the Coolie understood. He understood too quickly.

SCENE 4

A CONVERSATION IN DANGEROUS
TERRITORY

COOLIE (*singing*):
    Urga, Urga
    I am on my way to Urga.
    Nothing can stop me now:
    Bandits cannot keep me from Urga
    The desert cannot keep me from Urga
    For there's food in Urga
    And pay.

MERCHANT: This Coolie isn't worried, oh no! There are
    bandits in this part of the country — the station at-
    tracts all sorts of rabble. And he sings! (*To the*
    COOLIE:) I never did like that Guide. One day in-
    subordinate, the next licking my boots. Not an honest
    man.

COOLIE: Yes, Master. (*Singing again:*)
    Urga, Urga
    The road is hard to Urga
    I hope my feet hold up
    For there's rest in Urga
    And pay.

MERCHANT: Now just why do you sing? What are you so
    cheery about, my friend? You really aren't afraid of
    robbers? What they could take doesn't belong to you,
    what *you* have to lose belongs to me. That it?

COOLIE:
    Urga, Urga
    My wife awaits me in Urga
    Our little son awaits me. . . .

MERCHANT (*interrupting him*): I don't like that singing!
    We have no reason to sing. They can hear you all

121

the way to Urga. That's how to attract the attention of the rabble. Tomorrow you can sing as much as you want.

COOLIE: Yes, Master.

MERCHANT (*now walking in front of him*): He wouldn't defend himself for one second if anyone tried to take his things away. What would he do? If my property is in danger, it's his duty to defend it like his own. But he wouldn't. Never. A bad lot. He never says anything. That kind are the worst. I wish I could see into his mind. What's he planning to do? He has nothing to laugh about and he laughs. What at? Why, for instance, does he have me walk ahead of him? *He's* the one that knows the way. And where is he taking me? (*He looks around and sees the* COOLIE *wiping out their footprints in the sand.*) What's that you're doing?

COOLIE: Wiping out our footprints, Master.

MERCHANT: And why, may I ask?

COOLIE: On account of the bandits.

MERCHANT: I see, on account of the bandits. But I want it to be clear where you've taken me. Where *are* you taking me anyway? You go first!

The COOLIE *now walks in front of the* MERCHANT.

Silence. Then the MERCHANT *says to himself:*

In this sand our footprints really are very easy to see. Actually, of course, it would be a good thing to wipe out our footprints.

SCENE 5

AT THE RUSHING RIVER

COOLIE: We've been on the right road, Master. What we see there is the Myr river. In general, at this time of year, the river isn't hard to cross but, when it's in flood, the current is very strong, and you take your life in your hands.

MERCHANT: We must get across.

COOLIE: You often have to wait a week or so to get across safely. At present you take your life in your hands.

MERCHANT: We'll see about that. We can't wait a single day.

COOLIE: Then we'll have to look for a ford — or a boat.

MERCHANT: It takes too much time.

COOLIE: But I can't swim properly.

MERCHANT: The water isn't very high.

COOLIE (*lowers a stick in the water*): It is very high.

MERCHANT: Once you're in the water, you'll swim all right, you'll have to. You can't see the matter from all sides like me, know what I mean? Why must we get to Urga? Are you too much of a fool to understand it's doing mankind a service to extract oil from the earth? When the oil is extracted, there'll be railways here and prosperity will spread. There'll be bread and clothes and heaven knows what. And who will bring this about? *We* shall. It all depends on *our* journey. Just imagine: the eyes of the whole country are on you — a little man like you! And you hesitate to do your duty?

COOLIE (*has been nodding respectfully during this speech*):
I can't swim properly.

MERCHANT: I risk my life too.

The COOLIE *nods overawed.*

I don't understand you. Prompted by low considera-
tions of pecuniary gain, you have no interest in
reaching Urga as soon as possible. Your interest is
to get there as late as possible — because you're
paid by the day. In fact it isn't the journey that
interests you, it's the pay!

COOLIE (*stands hesitating at the river bank*): What am
I to do? (*He sings:*)

1.
Here is the river.
To swim across is dangerous.
Look: There are two men on the riverbank.
One swims across, the other
Hesitates.
Is the first brave? The second cowardly?
No: On the other side
One of the two has business.

2.
The first emerges with a smile from the dangerous
    water
Onto the opposite bank which he has conquered:
He now sets foot on his property and eats new food.
The second emerges from the dangerous water
Into nothing:
Gasping, and weaker than before, he now confronts
New dangers.
So:
Are both brave?
Are both wise?
They conquered the river together but
They are not both conquerers.

3.
WE and YOU AND I
Are not the same thing.
WE defeat the foe
But YOU defeat ME.

At least let me rest for half a day. I'm tired from all the carrying. Maybe after a rest, I *can* get across.

MERCHANT: I know a better solution: You'll get my revolver in your back. Shall we bet you get across? (*He pushes him on. To himself.*) My money makes me fear bandits and overlook the dangerous state of the river (*He sings:*)

This is how man masters the desert and the rushing
    river.
This is how man masters man.
The oil, the oil we need, is his reward.

SCENE 6

THE BIVOUAC

It is evening, and the COOLIE, *whose arm is broken, is trying to pitch the tent. The* MERCHANT *is sitting nearby.*

MERCHANT: But I told you, you don't need to put the tent up today — after breaking your arm crossing the river.

The COOLIE *goes on putting it up and does not speak.*

If I hadn't pulled you out of the water you'd have drowned.

The COOLIE *goes on.*

Though of course, I am not responsible for your accident — the tree might just as easily have hit *me* — all the same the mishap befell you during a journey in my company. I have very little cash on me. My bank is in Urga. When we arrive, I'll give you some money.

COOLIE: Yes, Master.

MERCHANT: He doesn't waste words. And with every look he gives me to understand that I'm the cause of his misfortune. A malicious lot, these coolies! (*To the* COOLIE:) You can lie down. (*He walks away and sits down at a distance.*) It's clear that his mishap makes more difference to me than to him. The rabble don't much bother whether they're cripples or men. So long as they can eat, they're satisfied. Their natural limitations keep them from bothering their heads about themselves any further. They're failures. Now, if you make something and it turns out a failure you throw it away. They, *being* failures, throw themselves away. It's the hundred percenter who fights (*He sings:*)

126

Sick men die
But strong men fight:
   And that's how it should be.
All power to the strong
No power to the weak:
   For that's how it should be.
Things that fall, let 'em fall,
Then give 'em a kick:
   Isn't that how it should be?
Who wins the battle
Can sit down to dine:
   Yes, that's how it should be.
The conqueror's cook
Makes no count of the slain:
   And that's how it should be.
And God up in heaven
God of things as they are
He made master and man:
   And that's how it should be.
Who has good luck is good,
Who has bad luck is bad:
   That's just how it should be.

The COOLIE *has approached. The* MERCHANT *notices him and is startled.*

He's been listening! Stop! Stay where you are! What do you want?

COOLIE: The tent is ready, Master.

MERCHANT: Don't sneak about in the night. I don't like it. When a man comes to me, I like to hear his footsteps. And I want to look him in the eye when I talk to him. You lie down, and don't trouble yourself so much about me.

The COOLIE *goes back.*

Stop! You go into the tent! I'll sit here because I'm used to the fresh air.

The COOLIE *goes into the tent.*

I wish I knew how much he heard of my song. (*Pause.*) What's he doing now? He's still busy.

The COOLIE *is seen carefully preparing his "bed."*

COOLIE: I hope he doesn't notice anything. With one arm, I can't cut grass properly.

MERCHANT: Stupid not to be on guard. To trust people is stupid. Through me, this man has been hurt — possibly handicapped for the rest of his life. From his point of view, it's only right if he pays me back. And a strong man asleep is no stronger than a weak man asleep. Men shouldn't have to sleep! Certainly it would be better to sit in the tent. In the open you're a prey to every sort of sickness. But what sickness could be as dangerous as this man is! He walks at my side for little money — and I have much money — and the road is equally difficult for us both. When he was tired, he was beaten. When the guide sat down with him, the guide was dismissed. When he wiped out footprints in the sand — perhaps really because of bandits — he was treated with suspicion. When he showed fear at the river, he was given my revolver to look at. How can I sleep in the same tent with such a man? He can't make me believe he'll just put up with it all! I'd like to know what he's thinking up in there now!

The COOLIE *is seen peacefully lying down to sleep.*

I'd be a fool to go into the tent!

SCENE 7
THE END OF THE ROAD
A

MERCHANT: What are you stopping for?

COOLIE: Master, the road ends here.

MERCHANT: Well?

COOLIE: Master, if you beat me, don't beat me on my sore arm. I don't know the way from here on.

MERCHANT: But the man at Station Han explained it to you.

COOLIE: Yes, Master.

MERCHANT: When I asked you if you understood him, you said yes.

COOLIE: Yes, Master.

MERCHANT: And you did not understand him?

COOLIE: No, Master.

MERCHANT: Then why did you say yes?

COOLIE: I was afraid you'd throw me out. I only know it's supposed to be along the water holes.

MERCHANT: Then go along the water holes.

COOLIE: But I don't know where they are.

MERCHANT: Get moving! And don't try to make a fool of me. I know you've traveled this road before.

They walk on.

COOLIE: But wouldn't it be better to wait for that other caravan?

129

MERCHANT: No.

They walk on.

THE SHARED WATER
B

MERCHANT: Where do you think you're going now? That's north, the east is *there!*

The COOLIE *proceeds in that direction.*

Stop! What's the matter with you?

The COOLIE *stops but does not look at the* MERCHANT.

Why don't you look me in the eyes?

COOLIE: I thought the east was there.

MERCHANT: Just you wait, my lad! I'll show you how to guide me. (*He beats him.*) Do you know now where the east is?

COOLIE (*screaming*): Not on that arm.

MERCHANT: Where's the east?

COOLIE: There.

MERCHANT: And where are the water holes?

COOLIE: There.

MERCHANT (*furious*): There? But you were going *there!*

COOLIE: No, Master.

MERCHANT: Aha! So you were not going there? Were you going *there?* (*He beats him.*)

COOLIE: Yes, Master.

MERCHANT: Where are the water holes?

The COOLIE *is silent. The* MERCHANT *seems calm.*

You said just now you know where the water holes are? *Do* you know?

The COOLIE *is silent.*

MERCHANT (*beating him*): Do you know?

COOLIE: Yes.

MERCHANT (*beating him*): Do you know?

COOLIE: No.

MERCHANT: Give me your flask.

The COOLIE *gives it to him.*

I could now take the view that all the water belongs to me because you guided me wrong. But I won't! (*To himself:*) I forgot myself: I oughtn't to have beaten him in this situation.

C *

MERCHANT: We were here before. Look, our footprints!

COOLIE: When we were here we must have been near the right road.

MERCHANT: Pitch the tent. Our flask is empty, there's nothing left. (*The* MERCHANT *sits down while the* COOLIE *pitches the tent. The* MERCHANT *drinks secretly out of his bottle. To himself:*) He mustn't notice that I still have something to drink. Otherwise, if he's got a spark of understanding in his thick skull, he'll do me in. If he comes close, I shoot. (*He takes out his revolver and places it on his knee.*) If we could only reach the last water hole! I'm nearly strangled with thirst. How long can a man stand thirst?

---

* Section *C* has no title in the 1937 text.

COOLIE: I must hand over to him the flask that the Guide
at the Station gave me. Otherwise, if they find us,
me still alive and him half dead, they'll put me on
trial.

He takes the bottle and walks toward the MERCHANT.
The MERCHANT *suddenly discovers the* COOLIE *in
front of him and doesn't know if the* COOLIE *has
seen him drink or not. The* COOLIE *has not seen him
drink. In silence, he holds out the flask to him. But
the* MERCHANT, *thinking that it is one of the big
stones of the countryside and that the* COOLIE, *en-
raged, wants to kill him, cries out loudly.*

MERCHANT: Put that stone down!

*And with a single shot from his revolver he brings
down the* COOLIE *who, not understanding, continues
to hold out the flask.*

I was right. There, you bastard! You had it coming.

The Song of the Tribunals

*Sung by the actors while the stage is set for the trial
scene.*

In the wake of the robber hordes
Come the tribunals
And when the innocent are murdered
The judges gather about their corpses and condemn
   them.
At the grave of the murdered
All their rights are murdered.
The words of the tribunal
Fall like the shadow of a knife
And the knife, alas, is sufficient:
What need, afterward, of a verdict?
Overhead fly the vultures and whither?
The desert has repelled them:
The tribunals will feed them.

Here the assassin will find a home
And the persecutor a sanctuary.
Here the thief hides what he has stolen
And wraps it in a piece of paper upon which
A law is written.

SCENE 8

THE TRIBUNAL

The GUIDE, *the Coolie's* WIDOW, *and the* INNKEEPER *are already sitting in the courtroom.*

GUIDE (*to the* WIDOW): Are you the Coolie's Widow? I am the Guide who engaged your husband. I've heard you are demanding the punishment of the Merchant and damages. I came to this law court right away because I have proof that your husband was innocent. It's in my pocket.

INNKEEPER (*to the* GUIDE): I hear you have a proof in your pocket. Let me give you some advice: leave it in your pocket.

GUIDE: Is the Coolie's Widow to go away empty-handed?

INNKEEPER: Do you want to be blacklisted?

GUIDE: I'll think it over.

The JUDGE *and his two colleagues take their seats. So does the accused* MERCHANT. *Also the* INNKEEPER *and the members of the second caravan.*

JUDGE: I declare the proceedings open. The Widow of the deceased has the floor.

WIDOW: My husband carried this gentleman's baggage through the Jahi desert. Shortly before the end of the journey, his master shot him down. Even though my husband can't be brought back to life thereby, I demand that his murderer be punished!

JUDGE: You are also demanding damages.

WIDOW: Yes. My little son and myself have lost our breadwinner.

134

JUDGE (*to the* WIDOW): The material part of the claim is nothing to be ashamed of. I'm not reproaching you for it. (*To the members of the second caravan:*) Behind the expedition of the merchant Karl Langmann came another expedition — joined by the guide who had been dismissed from the first expedition. They sighted the stranded expedition barely a mile from the route. What did you see as you approached?

LEADER (*of the second caravan*): The Merchant had very little water left in his flask. And his carrier lay dead on the sand.

JUDGE (*to the* MERCHANT): Did you shoot the man?

MERCHANT: Yes. He attacked me unawares.

JUDGE: How did he attack you?

MERCHANT: He intended to strike me down from behind with a stone.

JUDGE: Can you explain the motive of his attack?

MERCHANT: No.

JUDGE: Did you drive your men very hard?

MERCHANT: No.

JUDGE: Is the guide present who made the first part of the journey and was dismissed?

GUIDE: Present!

JUDGE: What have you to say?

GUIDE: As far as I know, the important thing for the merchant was to be in Urga as soon as possible on account of a concession.

JUDGE (*to the* MERCHANT): Had you the impression that the expedition behind you maintained an unusually high speed?

MERCHANT: Not unusually. We had a full day's start and kept it up.

JUDGE (*to the* MERCHANT): Then you *must* have driven them hard.

MERCHANT: *I* didn't drive them hard. That was the Guide's job.

JUDGE (*to the* GUIDE): Did the accused make a point of telling you to drive the carrier especially hard?

GUIDE: I didn't drive him harder than the usual. Maybe less hard.

JUDGE: Why were you dismissed?

GUIDE: Because in the Merchant's opinion my attitude to the Coolie was too friendly.

JUDGE: And you shouldn't be so friendly? Did you have the impression that this Coolie who was not to be given friendly treatment was a malcontent?

GUIDE: No. He put up with everything because, as he told me himself, he was afraid of losing his job: he didn't belong to a union.

JUDGE: Did he have a lot to put up with? Answer! And don't be thinking over your answers all the time! The truth will out!

GUIDE: I was only with him as far as Station Han.

INNKEEPER (*to himself*): That's the way to talk to them.

JUDGE (*to the* MERCHANT): Did anything occur afterward that could explain the Coolie's attack?

MERCHANT: No. On my side, nothing.

JUDGE: My good fellow, don't paint yourself whiter than you really are, you won't get off that way. If you handled your Coolie with kid gloves on, how do you explain his hatred for you? Obviously, you can

only make us believe that you acted in self-defense
if you also make us believe in the Coolie's hatred.
Use your head!

MERCHANT: Let me confess this much: I did beat him
one time.

JUDGE: Aha! And you believe that such hatred on the
Coolie's part was occasioned by this one event?

MERCHANT: No. I let him have my revolver in his back
when he didn't want to cross the river. It's also true
that he broke his arm during the crossing. That too
was my fault.

JUDGE (*smiling*): In the Coolie's opinion.

MERCHANT (*also smiling*): Of course. Actually, I helped
him get out of the water.

JUDGE: Very well. *After* the dismissal of the guide you
gave the Coolie occasion to hate you. And before-
hand? (*To the* GUIDE, *insisting*:) Admit, after all,
that the man hated the Merchant! A moment's
thought makes it quite obvious. It stands to reason
that a man who is badly paid, who is forcibly driven
into danger, whose very health is impaired for another's gain, who risks his life for almost nothing —
it stands to reason that he should hate him!

GUIDE: He didn't hate him.

JUDGE: We would like now to cross-question the Innkeeper of Station Han. Perhaps his report will give
us an idea of the Merchant's relations with his personnel. (*To the* INNKEEPER:) How did the Merchant treat his men?

INNKEEPER: Well.

JUDGE: Shall I clear the court? Do you think it would hurt
your business if you tell the truth?

INNKEEPER: No. In the present case, it isn't necessary.

JUDGE: As you wish.

INNKEEPER: He even gave the Guide tobacco and paid his wages in full without making trouble. And the Coolie was well-treated too.

JUDGE: Your station is the last police station on this route?

INNKEEPER: Yes, that's where the uninhabited Jahi desert begins.

JUDGE: I see. This friendliness of the Merchant's was more or less imposed by circumstances, was not destined to last — a strategic friendliness, so to speak. It reminds me of our officers during the war. They made it their business to be kinder 'and kinder to their men the nearer they got to the front. Friendship of this sort doesn't count, of course.

MERCHANT: For example: he'd been forever singing along the way. From the moment when I threatened him with the revolver — to get him across the river — I never heard him sing again.

JUDGE: He must have been completely embittered. It stands to reason. Again I must refer to the war. In wartime one could understand the men saying to us officers: *You* fight for yourselves, but we fight for you! And likewise the Coolie could say to the Merchant: You do business for yourself, but I do business for you!

MERCHANT: Let me confess something else. When we got lost I shared one flask of water with him but I intended to drink the second myself.

JUDGE: Did he see you drinking maybe?

MERCHANT: I assumed he did — when he came toward me with the stone in his hand. I knew he hated me. When we came to uninhabited territory I was on guard day and night. I had to assume that he would fall on me at the first opportunity. If I hadn't killed him, he would have killed me.

WIDOW: I would like to say something. He can't have attacked him. He never attacked anybody.

GUIDE: Keep calm. I have proof of his innocence in my pocket.

JUDGE: Has the stone with which the Coolie threatened you been found yet?

LEADER: That man (*pointing to the* GUIDE) took it out of the dead man's hand.

The GUIDE *shows the flask.*

JUDGE: Is that the stone? Do you recognize it?

MERCHANT: Yes, that's the stone.

GUIDE: Then look what is in the stone. (*Pours water.*)

FIRST COLLEAGUE: It's a water flask and not a stone. He was handing you water.

SECOND COLLEAGUE: It certainly looks now as if he hadn't wanted to kill him at all.

GUIDE (*embracing the* WIDOW): You see now: I was able to prove it. He was innocent. It is exceptional but I was able to prove it. I gave him the flask when he set out from the last station. The Innkeeper is my witness: this is my flask.

INNKEEPER (*to himself*): Fool! Now *he's* done for!

JUDGE: That cannot be the truth. (*To the* MERCHANT:) Are we to believe he gave you something to drink?

MERCHANT: It must have been a stone.

JUDGE: No, it was not a stone. You can see for yourself it was a flask.

MERCHANT: But I couldn't *assume* it was a flask. The man had no reason to give me something to drink. I wasn't his friend.

GUIDE: But he did give him something to drink!

JUDGE: But why did he give him something to drink? Why?

GUIDE: I suppose because he thought the Merchant was thirsty.

The judges exchange smiles.

Probably because he was human.

The judges smile.

Perhaps because he was stupid — I think he had nothing against the Merchant.

MERCHANT: Then he must have been *very* stupid. The man had been hurt through me, possibly for the rest of his life. His arm. It was only right if he wanted to pay me back.

GUIDE: It was only right.

MERCHANT: He walked at my side for little money — and I have much money. But the road was equally difficult for us both.

GUIDE (*to himself*): So he knows!

MERCHANT: When he was tired he was beaten.

GUIDE: And that was wrong?

MERCHANT: To assume that the Coolie would not strike me down at the first opportunity would have been to assume he had lost his reason.

JUDGE: You mean you assumed with justification that the Coolie must have had something against you. You may, then, have killed a man who possibly was harmless — because you couldn't *know* him to be harmless. This happens also with the police at times. They shoot into a crowd of demonstrators — quite peaceful folk — because they can't see why these folk don't simply drag them off their horses and lynch them. Actually, the police in such cases fire out

of pure fear. And that they are afraid is proof of
their good sense. You mean you couldn't know the
Coolie was an exception!

MERCHANT: One must go by the rule, not by the exception.

JUDGE: Exactly. What reason could this Coolie have had
to give his tormentor something to drink?

GUIDE: No sensible reason.

JUDGE (*singing*):
Such is the rule: an eye for an eye.
Only a fool waits for an exception.
A man of sense would not expect
Something to drink from his enemy.

GUIDE:
For in the system which they created
Humanity is an exception:
If you perform a human act
You pay the penalty.
O fear for the man
Who would be friendly:
If he tries to help someone, hold him back.
Near at hand someone is thirsty:
Close your eyes, quick!
And close your ears!
Near at hand someone is groaning:
Don't make a move!
Someone's shouting for help.
Woe to you
If you forget this!
You give a man something to drink
And it's a wolf that drinks.

JUDGE: The Court takes counsel. (*The* JUDGE *and his*
TWO COLLEAGUES *withdraw*.)

LEADER (*of the second caravan*): Aren't you afraid of
never getting another job?

GUIDE: I had to tell the truth.

LEADER (*smiling*): Well, if you had to . . .

The judges return.

JUDGE (*to the* MERCHANT): The Court has another question to put to you. Is it possible that you had something to gain by shooting the Coolie?

MERCHANT: On the contrary. I needed him for the business on hand in Urga. He carried the maps and surveying instruments which I needed. I could never have carried all those things by myself.

JUDGE: Then you didn't close the deal in Urga?

MERCHANT: Of course not. I was too late. I am ruined.

JUDGE: Then I pronounce the verdict. The Court regards it as proven that the Coolie approached his master not with a stone but with a water flask. But even when this is granted, it is more credible that the Coolie wished to kill his master with the flask than that he wished to give him something to drink. The carrier belonged to a class which has indeed motive to feel itself handicapped. For men like the Coolie it was nothing short of good sense to protect himself against an unequal distribution of the water. Yes, to these people with their narrow and one-sided outlook, moreover, that embraces only the external realities, it must even seem just to avenge oneself on one's tormentor. On the day of reckoning they have everything to gain. The Merchant did not belong to the same class as his carrier. He had therefore to expect the worst from him. The Merchant could not believe in an act of comradeship on the part of a carrier whom, as he has confessed, he had brutalized. Good sense told him he was threatened in the highest degree. The uninhabited character of the territory must perforce have filled him with apprehension. The absence of police and laws made it possible for his employee to seize his share of the water — nay, encouraged him to do so. The accused acted, therefore, in justifiable self-defense — it being a matter of indifference whether he was threatened or must *feel* himself threatened. In the circumstances he had to feel himself threatened. The accused is therefore acquitted. The plea of the carrier's widow is dismissed.

THE ACTORS:

So ends
The story of a journey
You have heard and you have seen
You have seen what is common, what continually occurs
But we ask you:
Even if it's not very strange, find it estranging
Even if it is usual, find it hard to explain
What here is common should astonish you
What here's the rule, recognize as an abuse
And where you have recognized an abuse
Provide a remedy!

APPENDIX

Salzburg Dance of Death

INTRODUCTION

WHEN BERTOLT BRECHT appeared before the House Un-American Activities Committee in 1947, he had a plane ticket for Paris in his pocket, and right after being quizzed by Congressman J. Parnell Thomas he flew to Europe and settled for a while near Zurich. He might even have stayed in Switzerland indefinitely, except that the Swiss authorities did not smooth out the way. As for Germany, he did not like the idea of living under a foreign military government, Eastern or Western. Dr. Benno Frank (now of the Cleveland Playhouse) tried to influence the American authorities toward making it attractive for Brecht to return to his native Bavaria, but to no avail.

To the cottage near Zurich came Brecht's old friend Caspar Neher, the stage designer. His home was in Salzburg, where he knew the people connected with the Festivals. One of these, the composer Gottfried von Einem, wished to interest Brecht in the Festivals. He even dreamed that what Max Reinhardt had been Bertolt Brecht would become. So von Einem also visited Brecht, and made an impression. The Brechts then visited Salzburg, looked things over, considered buying a house there, talked of possible theatrical projects in Salzburg and Vienna. It was agreed that *Antigone, Mother Courage* and *The Caucasian Chalk Circle* were all plays that might be done in the one city or both. 1949 was to be "Goethe Year," and Brecht would make a four-hour stage version of the two parts of *Faust* with Fritz Kortner or Peter Lorre in the title role. . . .

It was in April, 1949, that Brecht came up with an idea that has since caused raised eyebrows. An alternative to Switzerland and both Germanies had occurred to him: his wife, Helene Weigel, was Austrian; why couldn't he, as her husband, acquire Austrian citizenship? The question was addressed to von Einem, and answered. The machinery was set in motion. Brecht filled out forms and wrote letters to the right VIPs. It is interesting that one of the three references he gave was "Albert Einstein, Princeton." And one wonders how deeply his tongue was implanted in his cheek when he put into letters such things as:

> My longing [*Sehnsucht*] for Austria is in no way to be attributed to external circumstances. The explanation is that, being fifty years old, I would like to do intellectual [*geistig*] work in a land that offers the appropriate atmosphere for it. This is Austria. . . .

and:

> Let me stress that I feel myself to be only a poet and wish to serve no definite political ideology, nor do I wish to be regarded as the exponent of such an ideology. I reject the idea of repatriating myself in Germany. . . .

The Austrian citizenship came through in 1950, and Brecht was to die, six years later, an Austrian. But as early as December, 1948, he had traveled to East Berlin, via Prague, to stage *Mother Courage*. A relatively short trip in itself, this laid the basis for his future and famous work in the divided German capital. Just when it became certain that Brecht was in Berlin for life is not clear. But it is clear when his Salzburg plans finally fell through. His acquisition of Austrian citizenship had been private to the point of secrecy. But in the summer of 1951, the secret got into the papers. There was something of a scandal, in that the notorious German Red, now happily settling, it seemed, in East Germany, had just been granted citizenship in virtuous Austria. Brecht wrote to von Einem:

> Cas [Neher] tells me, and I note it in the papers, too, that you have now landed in difficulties as a result of your willingness to help me. Tell me at once if you need any statements or letters from me. Shall I send you some pages of the *Salzburg Dance of Death?* The conception is ready. I don't understand how anyone

can take it amiss that you as an artist have helped another artist — after all, I had no papers at all at the time! Warmly, your old Bertolt Brecht.

The *Salzburg Dance of Death* was Brecht's gift — or bribe, if you will — to the Austrian authorities. They were to give him a passport, and he was to write them a play. It bore, of course, a sting in its tail — a play in their own manner, if not after their own hearts, a play that could be announced on the same program as Hofmannsthal's *Everyman*. It might even have ousted the Hofmannsthal piece from the program. In one's wildest dreams one can imagine a Salzburg Brechtianized through and through, a Salzburg that had become East Berlin and was performing the collected works of Brecht, plus selected classics, these, also, thoroughly Brechtianized. It is, of course, a Salzburg without Austrians, if not without Austrian passports, and, if it is not also a Salzburg without an international public, it is a Salzburg with an international clientele never seen hitherto among the paunches and the *Lederhosen*.

One cannot help wishing the dream had come true. All that remains of it is these five tiny fragments. But from two of Brecht's letters to von Einem, one gets a pretty clear notion of what the completed play would have been like. The first of these letters (dated 1949) summarized his scheme:

> The Emperor's contract with Death. Death would set a limit to the number of victims of the next war and spare the Emperor and his entourage if they made him the sign agreed on. Forgetting of the sign because Death is so busy. Moral: You can't make deals with Death.

In 1951, he had this to add:

> . . . I have discovered that a second plot [in addition to the Emperor-Death plot] is needed, in which man is more closely seen. I have now sketched this plot. When the Emperor breaks off the crusade and returns to Salzburg, the Sultan's army does not follow him

because it also has been annihilated. Moreover, the great Death has set in and the Plague follows on the Emperor's heels. The second plot takes place in the family of the merchant Fruehwirt. Widow Fruehwirt has heard that a strange sickness is raging in Hungary and the peasants are selling their cattle dirt cheap. She sends her brother-in-law there to buy cheap. The brother-in-law catches the sickness, sees that he was sent away to make deals with Death, and hurries back, sick as he is, thus bringing the Plague into the house of the Fruehwirts. It is carnival season. Frau Fruehwirt's long-time servant, an old maid, escapes death by plague because she finds the strength to go to the carnival against her Mistress's orders.

I should like to add that my chief source for this brief report is an article by Siegfried Melchinger in the *Stuttgarter Zeitung* of January 5, 1963. I myself was seeing a good deal of Brecht in the years 1948-1951, but did not learn nearly as much about the *Dance of Death* as is told in Melchinger's article. However, I do recall Brecht giving a summary of the Emperor-Death plot in conversation. The conversational version went somewhat like this:

Rich people cannot understand why they die: it seems unfair. So they go to Death and say, "Couldn't something be worked out? Surely there are enough poor people to keep you busy." Death says, "All right," so long as they will make it clear to him, when he approaches on professional business, which *are* the rich ones. A sign is agreed on, and for a while the new system works well. The poor die and the rich bid fair to be immortal. But they have overlooked one small point: Death has a bad memory. How should he not have? There are so many poor people to have die. And now watching out for the sign given by the rich takes up time and attention. Death does not manage to maintain the efficiency of the early days of his compact. One day he lets a rich man die. Receiving the indignant protests of the still-living rich, he makes a slight effort. It is no good. He is on the downward path, and soon is as indiscriminate as in the past. You can't make deals with Death . . .

Sadly incomplete as a play, these outlines, plus the fragments that follow, seem to me to constitute a sufficient scenario for a ballet with words, on the lines of *The Seven Deadly Sins*. What a great dance could be made from the Breughelian meeting of the Carnival and the Plague!

— E.B.

CHARACTERS

Death

Three Carpenters

Builder

Emperor

Frau Fruehwirt

Mette

1.

DEATH *goes his rounds;* THREE CARPENTERS *building a bridge; their partner is* DEATH.

DEATH:
> Up with those beams! And speedily!

CARPENTER:
> Master, that's too much work for three.

DEATH:
> Time is money. Go, go, go!

CARPENTER:
> Not for us it isn't, though.

DEATH:
> No jokes! And while you're at it, sing!
> You'll make it without even noticing.

CARPENTER (*singing*):
> The early bird finds the worm, they say, Heave-ho!
> But the rich bird snatches the worm away, Heave-ho!

DEATH:
> Ts, ts, ts. Your songs give me quite a jolting.
> I find them revolting.
> Their attitude toward me is such
> That I can't be expected to like them much.
> Nothing in them but hate, hate, hate!
> Now a little song like this would be great:
> "To be happy you need not be king or lord,
> For labor is its own reward!"
> You there, Cheeseface, bend down, yes, bend!
> Your courage seems to be at an end.
> Bend down, no shirking, you poltroon!
> Or home you go without wages, and soon!

SECOND CARPENTER:
> And if I bend and do not shirk,

Feet-first you'll send me home from work.

BUILDER (*coming over*): What goes on?

DEATH:
> The same old thing. Only the whip
> Can induce human beings to let 'er rip.
> This building job, the way you go about it,
> Does it make sense, Builder? I doubt it.
> You use many planks. They cost many a guilder.
> A third of these planks would do, eh, Builder?
> Let me jump on them, let me stamp on them all!
> (*He leaps up onto the bridge and stamps on the
> planks.*)
> See for yourself! The bridge doesn't fall!

BUILDER:
> I'm grateful for the advice, I'm sure,
> But the bridge is for the Emperor.
> We're not economizing on it
> 'Cause everyone will ride upon it
> Who comes to the Emperor from afar.
> Our engineers, then, are particular;
> Except that the Emperor's visitors are few
> I'd use even more beams than I do.

DEATH:
> Let it be your bridge, then, not mine.
> I like to cut things fine.
> It's not as if arithmetic hadn't been invented yet!
> I'll go build houses in the slums instead.
> The Roof Over Your Head's my *spécialité*.
> Four beams, thin as a child's arm, stuck up with clay,
> Walls eggshell thin — such are my calculations!
> Everything according to the specifications!
> Arithmetic I just adore.
> This job here, Builder, is a bloody bore.

He goes angrily away, throwing away the blueprints.

2.

From Death's Speech to the Emperor

This year, Sire, has been rough:
My business is falling off.
I used to love my work. Of fun I had my fill.
Now I'm old before my time. I feel ill.
I am deceived and cheated,
Persecuted, defeated.
How cope with such catastrophes?
I've been having breathing difficulties.
Yes! There's no denying it. They occurred
When certain smells were smelled and certain sounds
    were heard.
It's gone so far that when I hear the jingle
Of gold in pockets, my very blood will tingle.
Or when the smell of bank-books hits my nose
Around my head I need wet clothes.
For cruel money — let me make this confession —
Is driving me right out of my profession.
When long ago the Good Lord said
I should change the living into the dead,
All men were equal, that's for sure.
There was no talk then of rich and poor.
It was not said a man might place
A bag of gold before my face
And buy me off with this same gold
Although he might be very old.
What'll they think of me, royal sir,
If I make distinctions of *this* caliber?
If I draw my tail in before some swine
With a lot of money and a palace fine —
While down the street, to make things worse,
I seize a good man with an empty purse?
They'll find me guilty of discrimination
And think me a corrupt abomination.

3.

The Emperor Answers Death's Speech on Bad Reputation

> Dear Goodman Death, calm down, pray do.
> Folk curse and swear about me, too.
> And they with difficulty see
> The difference between you and me.
> But if they go too far, then, drat 'em!
> The order of the day for us is: Up and at 'em!
> We'll stuff their snouts up. Do you ask
> With what we shall perform this task?
> Roast goose would serve
> Though it is more than they deserve.
> What those snouts have had coming since their birth
> Is a handful of earth.

4.

Interlude: Frau Fruehwirt's Bedroom

FRAU FRUEHWIRT:
> Mette, Mette, who knocks at the gate?*

METTE:
> Can't hear! I'm tending the fire in the grate.

FRAU FRUEHWIRT:
> There was something urgent about it, I know.

METTE:
> But who would come before the cockcrow?

FRAU FRUEHWIRT:
> Not my husband, he would wait till it's light.
> He'd never come riding home by night.
> That knocking again below! Mette, hark!

---

* The summary cited above indicates that it is the brother-in-law returning with the plague. In the summary Frau Fruehwirt is a widow; in the text she has a living husband.

METTE:

> I only hear the house-dog bark.
> No, it's only barking, it's just whimpering.
> No trace of anyone visiting.

FRAU FRUEHWIRT:

> Mette, is it not Carnival time?
> Watch the maids and keep them in line.
> Some things I won't allow: don't let them whore
>   about.
> If I let them, they'd go to the window and stick their
>   bottoms out.
> But, Mette, my milk bath, pour away,
> For I shall walk in state today!
> Carnival's but once in the year.
> That knocking again, oh dear, oh dear!
> Mette, go down and look who's been
> Knocking and leaving pauses inbetween
> The knocks. He's knocking, For Heaven's sake,
> As if he himself were but half awake!

Mette leaves.

5.

Later in the Interlude: Carnival During the Plague

FRAU FRUEHWIRT:

> And this is the fun of the dancing feet.
> It's two different beats that they beat.
> Some like it short, some like it to last.
> Some like a slow walk, others one that is fast.
> Some like it soft, some hard, and all
> Have their role.
> To drum without fear
> This man shuts up his ear.
> Mette, let's dance,
> I with my Lorenz, you with your Hans.

Lady and maid dance in different steps.

You toward the kitchen, I toward the dining hall.
I in my shoe of silk, you in your sandal of straw.
What's a joy to the one is a nightmare to the other.
That's how it is today, that's how it'll be forever.

The drumming in the dining hall stops. Mette dances on alone.

APPENDIX

What Was He Killed For?

Neues Deutschland, the organ of the East German Communists, carried in its issue of December 15, 1965, an attack on "skepticism" by Alfred Kurella. The skepticism he was attacking was that of the dissident, anti-Ulbricht elements within East German Communism. To defend the orthodox. Party position against heterodoxy was no new job for this man. He was already performing it thirty-five years earlier, when Brecht's *The Measures Taken* was first produced. Martin Esslin called attention to that fact in his book on Brecht. But, it seems, Mr. Esslin had access only to certain quotations from the Kurella article. Here, published for the first time outside Russia, is the full text as given in *Literature of the World Revolution,* Number 5, Moscow, 1931, as translated from the original German in *Literatur der Weltrevolution,* Number 4, Moscow, 1931. Further particulars on Alfred Kurella will be found in a current German paperback, *Deutsche Schicksale* by Alfred Kantorowicz (Vienna: Europa Verlag, 1964). It will be noticed that Kurella's translator calls *Die Massnahme* "Strong Measures." The collaborators he mentions are Hanns Eisler, composer of the score to the play, and Slatan Dudow (or Dudov), a director and playwright.

—E.B.

WHAT WAS HE KILLED FOR?

Criticism of the play *Strong Measures* by Brecht, Dudov and Eisler

Brecht's new play, which he produced in Germany in co-operation with Dudov and Eisler, has given rise to a lively discussion both in the bourgeois and the workers' press. This fact alone shows that it is a work of very much more than average importance. For this reason it is particularly necessary to give a true and searching criticism of this dramatic experiment. The play combines in a very original way the workers' choir, the talking choir, modern orchestral effects and epic drama.

The subject of the play is quite simple. Four agitators come before a Party tribunal, which is represented by a choir, to give an account of their illegal work in support of the Chinese Communist Party. Their work has been successful, but the agitators do not wish to accept the approval of the Party meeting before relating a certain incident. They themselves have had to shoot a fifth communist in order to carry out their task successfully. In order to bring out clearly the circumstances leading up to the shooting of their comrade the agitators reproduce before the Party meeting the main outlines of the events, each acting one of the parts. This acting is divided into different episodes and between each comments are made by the choir and there is argument and singing in which the specific principles that are involved are brought out.

The following episodes are reproduced: (1) How the young comrade who is afterwards shot comes to join the four agitators. (2) The preparation for illegal work; the putting on of a disguise, symbolizing the sinking of their personality. (3) The first false move on the part of the young comrade, who, out of pity, takes a step which betrays individualism and compromises the work. (4) The second false move on the part of the young comrade, who, from an idealist idea of justice does something which leads to an immature partial strike which is harmful to the mass movement. (5) The third false move on the part of the young comrade, who, from a feeling of decency breaks off his connections with the idealist of anti-imperialist convictions who is to supply him with arms for the uprising. (6) The fourth false move on the part of the young comrade, who under the pressure of the radical elements among the workers, who are impatient for an immediate uprising, infringes the discipline of the organization and disobeys the decisions of the Party, breaking out on his own into open fight; as in doing this he comes out into the open the four agitators shoot at him and make their way out of the town. (7 and 8). Just as the four agitators arrive at the frontier with the young wounded comrade, intending to send him across and thus reduce the risk of their being discovered, the situation in the town comes to such a head that the agitators have to go back again. They are followed. If they merely abandon the young comrade he will be searched by the police and in this way the secret of his participation in the work of the Bolshevist agitators will be discovered. The young comrade recognizes the difficulty of the situation and agrees to their shooting him and covering up all traces by throwing him into a pit. In the 9th and last episode the choir expresses its approval of this action, since through it the desired aim was attained, namely the success of the revolution.

The authors call their production a didactic play. This subheading agrees with Brecht's view that art is only a branch of pedagogy. As the program promises, the play aims at showing the wrong way of doing things in order to teach the spectator the right way. Thus the word "didactic" which is applied to the play should be taken in a literal sense.

One has to assume that the young comrade is a personi-
fication of the wrong course of action and that the agitators
give an example of the true bolshevism which everyone
should learn. This aim, which the authors have set themselves in presenting the play, demands a criticism which
shall examine very carefully the kind of ideology that is
concealed by them in this "didactic performance."

The first and most simple question that arises is: was
the young comrade wrong in the course he took and were
the agitators right? And it is just here that the difficulty
arises which the authors try to hide. The setting which the
authors took for their play (the Chinese revolution, the
rising up of the masses, the Union of Coolies, the anti-
imperialist movement, the Chinese capitalists, the Chinese
Communist Party, the Bolshevist Party of the Soviet Union,
etc.) is an actual historical setting. But in spite of this the
authors assert that the setting is imaginary and that they
have only selected here and there certain details from the
actual historical events. We cannot agree with the authors,
however, that their setting is imaginary. We cannot look
upon it as merely a convenient site for an ideological field
day which can be altered at will so as to serve the purpose
of demonstrating certain definite ideas. Such an artificial
limitation of the field is quite inadmissible for the simple
reason that the authors wrote their play not merely for the
sake of writing but for a definite public, a definite section
of the workers' movement to whom the circumstances of
the Chinese revolution and other events made use of in
the play are, in main outline, familiar, and amongst whom
these circumstances give rise to a very definite set of asso-
ciations.

In thus giving our opinion as to whose action can be
looked upon as right and whose wrong and as to what our
attitude should be to the didactic function of the play, we
shall start from the assumption that the events take place
against the perfectly real background of the Chinese revolution. If then we examine the behavior of the young

comrade and the three agitators from this point of view we shall find that it is just the young comrade who represents the point of view of the consistent revolutionary and Bolshevik, while the course taken by the agitators serves as an excellent example of the policy which, in the language of the Third International, is called the right opportunist tendency, for advocating which more than one communist has been excluded from the Party. In order to make this clearer we shall resort to the following artifice. We shall replace the young comrade and the three agitators with actual personalities from the period of the struggle inside the German Communist Party of the year 1923 when the mistakes made by the opportunists led to the defeat of the revolutionary movement. We shall quote from the events in Saxony.

HESSE: There is something about which I must inform you. The new unemployed leaders have been to see me and they have convinced me that we must immediately start the uprising. We must begin distributing propaganda leaflets at once with a call to an immediate general strike.

BRANDLER, TALHEIMER, RADEK: You have already failed us four times.

HESSE: The unemployed are coming out into the streets and want to destroy the spinning machines.

BRANDLER, TALHEIMER, RADEK: New revolutionary paths are opening up, our responsibilities are increasing, and yet you want to go on hanging up propaganda leaflets on the doors.

HESSE: The unemployed can't wait any longer. I can't either. There are too many people in the last straits of poverty.

BRANDLER, TALHEIMER, RADEK: On the other hand there are too few fighters.

HESSE: We have seven men who have come on behalf of the unemployed. Seven thousand men stand behind them.

TALHEIMER: But do you know what forces the government have at their disposal?

HESSE: No.

BRANDLER: Then you know too little. Where are your arms?

HESSE (showing his hands): We'll fight with tooth and nail.

BRANDLER, TALHEIMER, RADEK: That's not enough. Remember that according to the decisions of the Party together with the congress of factory committees which lead the working masses, the armed uprising has been put off until the delegates from Hamburg, Upper Silesia and the Ruhr district have arrived in the town.

We have chosen Saxony in 1923 because the German worker for whom the play was written knows very well from his own experience that to advocate a point of view such as that of the three agitators means virtually to support right-wing opportunism. This opportunism consists in an underestimation of the readiness of the masses for the revolutionary fight. Opportunism is also shown in the subordination of the Party to the organization that it ought to be leading (For Coolie Union, read congress of workers). Finally, it is quite a false view to hold that arms must be obtained before the fight can be started instead of that they should be fought for and won in the course of the struggle, as also that no move should be made until an agreement has been entered into with the other districts. It was just this opportunist attitude which led to the revolutionary movement being smothered.

We could give many instances of the Bolsheviks and Lenin having acted, in corresponding circumstances, in exactly the same way as the young comrade. It is impossible from any reasonable point of view to detach oneself from the great spontaneous revolutionary movement of the masses, one must start guiding this movement even when there is no certainty of its leading to victory. A classic example of this was the "July days" in Leningrad in 1917 and the rising in Moscow in 1905. Menshevist right-wing opportunism was against the rising. Plekhanov pronounced his now famous formula "It is no good fighting for your weapons!" against which Lenin brought the full weight of his revolutionary theory. So as not to be accused of wandering from the subject of the Chinese revolution we may cite the instance of the rising in Canton, which was discountenanced by the right-wingers but approved of by the Third International, in spite of the fact that it had criticisms to make about certain false steps taken by the Party leaders.

A right opportunist point of view can be traced like a colored thread right through Brecht's presentation of the young comrade's mistakes. Right-wing opportunism is also betrayed by setting the propaganda of the agitators, which one might call abstract, theoretical propaganda, over against those personal urges which the young comrade follows instinctively and perhaps in certain individual circumstances erroneously. Right-wing opportunism is also seen in the condemnation of the partial strike in the textile factory, a strike that the young comrade calls in the course of his open activities against the police. The inability of the agitators to lead the strikers is also a result of their opportunist tendencies. Instead of guiding it along revolutionary lines they allow it to be suppressed by the Coolie Union. The only mistake of the young comrade which one can really condemn is his attitude to the rice merchant who apparently represents the position of the Kuomintang. However, in order to settle this point one would have to know at what period of the Chinese revolution this event took place and whether or no the young comrade's class instincts told him that a break with the Kuomintang, which had gone over to the camp of the imperialists, had now become a historical necessity.

Now what is the explanation of the fact that the authors

have started out along one path but found themselves on another; that with the intention of writing an instructive Bolshevist play they have succeeded in producing an opportunist one? In order to answer this question we shall follow the whole chain of mistakes made by the authors, tracing them to their philosophico-ideological origins.

In order to make their ideas concrete the authors have created an artifical setting. They have not taken, as Lenin demands that they should, all the varied genuinely revolutionary situations from the dialectic materialists in order to show them in all their aspects with all their affinities and causal connections. They have taken odd pieces of reality in order to make from them a boundaried field for carrying out maneuvers with the ideas which they wish to demonstrate. They have acted to a certain extent like the amateur gods who try to create worlds starting from ideas. In other words they have approached reality and their material, idealistically (in the philosophical use of the word). This too is not merely by chance, for the idealist standpoint is apparent throughout the whole play. It is particularly noticeable in the way communism and the Communist Party are depicted. Communism is for the authors an idea which is to be found in the "doctrine of the classics." It is this that for them gives it its strength. The doctrine of the classics is the basis of the Party. When Brecht's *Strong Measures* praises the Party (such passages have genuine beauty from the poetical and musical point of view) and demands a sinking of personal aims in those of the Party, this is only because the Party incarnates a doctrine. The following statement is to be found in the text:—

"Individuality may be annihilated but the Party can never be annihilated because it rests on the doctrine of the classics."

From the point of view of the authors the indestructibility of the Party rests on the doctrine of the classics, and not on the fact that it represents the proletariat, the rising class, destined to come to power, which cannot be destroyed, since, if it was, the whole of society would return to barbarism.

We can now determine what are the class roots of this idealistic standpoint of the authors. Certain old survivals are evident in this way of thinking which is characteristic of the radical petty-bourgeois whom the chances of life have turned from the bourgeois camp into that of the proletariat. The petty-bourgeois, breaking away from the class in which he has been brought up defies its designation of communism as a senseless harlequinade of a crowd of bawling rowdies with the words, "No, communism provides the only true banner representing the highest knowledge of reality attained in our days." The petty-bourgeois revolutionary thinks that he has thus completely understood communism. He does not see that here it is impossible to separate theory from practice, that communism is a concrete, historically founded, militant class movement, that it is impossible to understand the communist doctrine and not throw in one's lot with the revolutionary movement.

This one-sided understanding of communism is so ingrained in Brecht that it colors his whole literary work. Brecht, the revolutionary dramatist who in his plays exhorts people to take up the communist ideas and even seeks to associate himself closely with the movement, has not yet succeeded in acquainting himself with the mass movement of the agitational-propagandist groups. These groups, however, give the true political setting for the creation of a revolutionary proletarian drama. Unless their experience is sufficiently assimilated the attempts of individual artists to create such a drama will prove futile. Brecht, on the other hand, supposes that it is quite sufficient to know the communist doctrine in order to create, like a scientist in his laboratory, revolutionary art.

As the ideological analysis which we have given of this play has shown, we are confronted with some obvious contradictions.

The play created a strong impression (and strong from

the revolutionary point of view) amongst a considerable section of the actors and the audience, whereas it was criticized (in some cases quite severely) by the bourgeois press. From this it follows that under certain, concrete historical conditions the play must be adjudged revolutionary. The bourgeois press took up the same attitude to it as to a Bolshevist play. How can this be accounted for?

Strong Measures forms a contrast to bourgeois art in that it represents an entirely new style. Its style distinguishes it from a bourgeois play and so it is looked upon as revolutionary. We emphasize this question of style rather than form. In passing from bourgeois to proletarian art we always notice this difference in style. Proletarian culture, which is the culture of a new class based on the activity of the great masses of the people, diverts art into new channels. But not only are new channels found; the function of art in social life itself is changed, as also the relations the different arts bear to one another and the kind of methods of which they make use.

It was also a wish to write something that would be a contribution to the young proletarian culture that moved the authors of *Strong Measures* purposely to break with the traditions of the bourgeois theater. Such an attempt, in itself, however wrongly it may have been carried out, deserves particular notice. *Strong Measures* will have a very important place in the future history of proletarian art, and even when the play is no longer produced (which will probably very soon be the case) its influence will be felt in the programs of propaganda theater troops.

The immediate revolutionary effect of *Strong Measures* is, however, not confined to this. In those parts where right ideas from the proletarian ideological arsenal are clearly formulated, the play passes very considerable artistic merit. Such songs as that in praise of illegal work, "The Song of Supply and Demand" (which would be better named The Song of Merchandise), and that in praise of the Party (omitting the ideological mistakes referred to above) must be ranked with some of the most important revolutionary works of the age, and they will long outlive the play as a whole.

Finally we must not forget that this work of a petty-bourgeois writer appears at a time when the campaign of calumny against the communists is assuming the most violent forms, at a time when many intellectuals who recently sympathized with communism are going over to the other side and when on the other hand new sections of the intelligentsia are joining its ranks. Such a play as *Strong Measures,* even in its present form, helps the latter forward. Thus from this point of view *Strong Measures* is in the long run a revolutionary gesture, and one which the proletariat must defend against its bourgeois detractors.

BIBLIOGRAPHICAL NOTES

THE JEWISH WIFE was first published as *Die jüdische Frau,* one of *Zwei Szenen aus dem Zyklus "Furcht und Elend des Dritten Reiches"* in *Das Wort* (Moscow), IV, 3, 1939. This English version first appeared in *The Nation,* September 11, 1943, and was reprinted in *The Private Life of the Master Race* (New Directions, 1944).

IN SEARCH OF JUSTICE was first published as *Rechtsfindung 1934* in *Das Wort* (Moscow), III, 6, 1938. This English version first appeared in *The Private Life of the Master Race,* as cited above.

THE INFORMER was first published as *Der Spitzel* in *Das Wort* (Moscow), III, 3, 1938. This English version first appeared in *Theatre Arts,* September, 1944, and was reprinted in *The Private Life of the Master Race* (New Directions, 1944).

THE ELEPHANT CALF was first published as *Das Elefantenkalb oder Die Beweisbarkeit jeglicher Behauptung* in the same volume as *Mann ist Mann,* Im Propylaen-Verlag, Berlin, copyright 1926 by Arcadia Verlag. This English version first appeared in *Evergreen Review,* Number 29 (1963), and was reprinted in the volume *Baal, A Man's A Man and The Elephant Calf,* Evergreen Black Cat Books, 1964.

THE MEASURES TAKEN was first published as *Die Massnahme* by G. Kiepenheuer, Berlin, copyright 1930.

Kiepenheuer reprinted it, with revisions, in the following year, in the *Versuche* series. It has subsequently appeared in the *Gesammelte Werke* of 1938 and the *Stücke* as published in the West by Suhrkamp and in the East by Aufbau. Eric Bentley translated the version in the *Gesammelte Werke* for *The Colorado Review*, Winter 1956-57, and this translation was reprinted in his *The Modern Theatre*, Volume Six (Doubleday Anchor, 1960). The present translation is based on the 1930 text. (Another translation, by Elizabeth Hanunian, was published by the U.S. Government in the records of the House Committee on UnAmerican Activities, 1947. This text was reprinted without change in Eric Bentley's *Thirty Years of Treason* [Viking Press, 1971].) Selections from Hanns Eisler's score for *The Measures Taken* are printed in *The Brecht Eisler Song Book*, distributed in the 1990s by Music Sales Corporation, 225 Park Avenue South, New York, NY 10003.

THE EXCEPTION AND THE RULE was first published as *Die Ausnahme und die Regel* in *Internationale Literatur* (Moscow), VII, 10, 1937. This English version first appeared in the little magazine *Chrysalis*, VII, 11-12, 1954, and was reprinted in *New Directions 15* (New Directions and Meridian Books, 1955).

The SALZBURG DANCE OF DEATH was first published as *Das Salzburger Totentanz* in the *Stuttgarter Zeitung*, January 5, 1963. This English version first appeared in the magazine *Portfolio*, Number 8, 1964, an affiliate of *Art News*. It was reprinted in the British magazine *Encore*, September-October, 1964.